Principles *of* Logo Design

Quarto.com

First published in 2022 by Rockport Publishers, an imprint of The Quarto Group,
100 Cummings Center, Suite 265-D, Beverly, MA 01915, USA.
T (978) 282-9590 F (978) 283-2742

Rockport Publishers titles are also available at discount for retail, wholesale, promotional, and bulk purchase. For details, contact the Special Sales Manager by email at specialsales@quarto.com or by mail at The Quarto Group, Attn: Special Sales Manager, 100 Cummings Center, Suite 265-D, Beverly, MA 01915, USA.

10 9 8 7

ISBN: 978-0-7603-7651-5

Digital edition published in 2022
eISBN: 978-0-7603-7652-2

Library of Congress Cataloging-in-Publication Data is available.

Design and Page Layout: George Bokhua
Illustrations, Images, and Photography: George Bokhua, except as indicated

Printed in China

Principles *of* Logo Design

A practical guide to creating effective signs, symbols, and icons

by George Bokhua

Contents

Chapter 3
Visual Matters

Preface

Creating something new and meaningful is not a simple skill that can be easily taught. This is certainly true in the case of logo design. Becoming a proficient designer requires abilities that develop only after years of practice and experimentation. A beginner whose goal is to be good must be prepared to invest significant time in learning design principles and working with the tools of logo creation. With study and experience, you can become a master of the research, mood boarding, and sketching skills required to execute effective logo designs.

We have instincts toward perfection and simplification. These are the primary creative forces that drive us to pay attention to details so relentlessly; any minor inconsistency becomes of the utmost importance. With prolonged practice of this "perfectionism," you will become able to identify the boundaries and push them further. The end goal of this obsession is discovering a new, more simple, more perfect, more timeless form of expression.

We must also learn to see nature and our surroundings as simple geometric forms. This practice enables you to start feeling a structure, a grid behind things. Once the structure and grid make sense, then composition makes sense, and then the design process becomes free, "effortless," and full of original surprises.

We must also become proud daydreamers who are constantly on the lookout for beautiful small shapes and compositions in our minds. Forms that initially appear in your imagination are mostly residue of daily visual inputs, the surface material that's too familiar and banal. However, the deeper you look into far, far galaxies, the more likely it is that you might see undiscovered shapes that need to be captured and depicted on paper.

A sketchbook and pencil are a designer's essential toolkit. I think of them as natural satellites, always with us and in easy reach for us to use. In logo design, the sketching process is foundational, and it offers certain freedoms that allow new shapes to be developed. Opening your mind to possibilities in this way can offer solutions that might not happen otherwise.

When we are fully engaged in thinking about design, snippets of concepts—and even the concepts themselves—can appear in the most unexpected moments. Whether you are on the subway, at a gym, or in a café, a designer must always be ready to take note of inspiration: it tends to slip away easily.

Taking photos is a handy tactic as well. For example, take notice of an exciting shape or of architecture that might be attention-grabbing. See how certain words in outdoor advertisements have interesting negative space shapes. As you are out walking and thinking, be open to moments when a visual suggestion appears from some everyday object. Any of these sources of inspiration has a chance to be turned into a design concept.

Last, resilience and the ability to stay on task are critical. In a certain sense, the logo design process should be viewed as sculpting. Lesser concepts and design solutions are chipped away, and stronger, more beautiful ones are solidified: a little bit to the left, a little bit to the right, adding and stripping some elements, and stripping some more. In a nutshell, that is what it's all about. A designer should not just stop when a particular result is achieved; you must keep adding and stripping elements. And the longer you stay in the process, the more correct and more perfect the final outcome becomes.

So as symbol makers, let us view ourselves as adventurers into the unknown, into the past and the future. Even better, as astronomers of imagination on a constant lookout for the places where simple, little beautiful shapes are waiting for us to be recognized, conceived, and made visible. After years of tireless journey in a timeless list of timeless symbols, one day, if we are lucky, we may hit the mark that finds home.

Chapter 1
General Concepts

Are Logos Just Logos?

In the modern world, logos are everywhere. They are like permanent satellites in our lives: some are as familiar to us as the Moon in the night sky, while others are as unknown as Jupiter's seventy-nine moons.

The logo or symbol plays a key role in establishing a connection between the consumer and a company. The relationship is similar to any human relationship. People love logos that evoke feelings of happiness, stability, confidence, and desirable memories. Behind the logo, and these personal associations, stands the company and the product itself.

The market is constantly trying to improve and adjust to the situation and time, based on the changing tastes of consumers. At the same time, in logo design adaptation must be done in a way that retains a sense of the logo's history, keeping it recognizable without limiting the next chapter of the company's development. Graphic designers have to shoulder this difficult task. Like other design fields, graphic design is always trendy.

An expert will easily recognize and identify symbols, logos, or signs and the respective decades when they were made. But beyond fashion and distinctiveness, we also encounter examples that have remained unchanged for many years. These are imprinted in our memory so thoroughly, as if the label itself, rather than the content, is the desired product. Chase Bank's logo was introduced in 1961 and, even as most forms of communication moved to the digital world, the symbol has not been changed a bit. The structure of the mark was designed in a way that easily transitioned to digital media without losing its crispness.

When creating a logo, the goal of the designer is to create a simple and durable chain reaction: it first goes on the business card, then emerges in a phone app, appears in the street—on the subway or a friend's bag, on book cover or product store bag. In each instance, the logo is easily recognizable. In each situation, it remains impressive and enduring.

Basic shapes from cave paintings that are still prevalent in modern logo design

1.618033

Along with all the positive qualities a good designer needs, it is crucial that we manage the complex process of design. Good results depend on this. And just like in math, there is a proper formula behind proper design.

Before we discuss invented and abstract formulas, let's focus first on the mathematical solution that already exists and is widely established in design: the Fibonacci Sequence. Two numbers—*a* and *b*—are in the golden ratio if their sum (*a* + *b*) divided by the larger number (*a*) is equal to the ratio of the larger number divided by the smaller number (*a*/*b*).

One can observe the golden ratio in a vast number of objects and phenomena, from mesmerizing spirals of smoke to the structures of shells, sunflowers, pinecones, hurricanes, DNA, and far galaxies. Some of the numbers are exactly in accordance with the ratio (1.6180339); others are very close. Nevertheless, the case is undeniable; there is the truth behind the number.

In the Fibonacci sequence, each subsequent number is equal to the sum of the previous two (0, 1, 1, 2, 3, 5, 8, 13, 21, and so on). The ratio of each number to the next is approximately 0.618. The ratio of each number to its predecessor is 1,618. Each subsequent number is 1,618 times larger than the previous one. The previous one represents 0.618 of the next.

More than simple arithmetic, the Fibonacci sequence is a rare mathematical operation used with joy and interest in ordinary life,

even by people who are not interested in mathematics. Fibonacci numbers can create unusual password combinations, and it is pleasant to be able to see and identify them in various objects or events.

At the first glance a shell, cone, sunflower, or a hand appears ordinary. But once you begin to notice them, the inexplicable and interesting behavior of Fibonacci numbers can have you looking for them everywhere: in your own photos, in movies, in museums and bad artists' salons, in book covers or logos.

When your search turns up something that is a match, or at least is close to the desired result, the object will always look better and inexplicably more interesting than it did before. No matter how overstated it may sound, people love numbers and happy mediums just as much as they hate math.

A swan logo using golden spiral as a structural base

A ram mark using golden spiral as a structural base

Rule or No Rule?

The famous Fibonacci sequence has captivated mathematicians, artists, designers, and scientists for centuries. The presence of a golden ratio in nature, architecture, art, and music is undeniable, but naturally, the numbers have their "fans" and antagonists. For some, the mathematical approach to art is seen as too cold and rational, too mechanistic.

Applying the golden ratio and Fibonacci sequence supports an easier understanding of good design. Use them whenever possible, as a valuable standard of organization. A mathematical approach, along with personal improvisations, can bring an order to the chaos that is rational, humanistic, and beautiful at the same time. However, math should not overshadow the original form or overpower a concept. If a form feels right, then numbers should not get in the way.

Enso sign, a universal symbol for simplicity, balance, and elegance

Less Is More?

Initially the catchphrase "less is more" had a simple meaning. First mentioned in Robert Browning's poem "Andrea del Sarto" (1855), it suggests that everything simple is better and more beautiful than the complex and tangled.

Nowadays this phrase is heard often—maybe even too often. But it's important to recognize that the way of thinking that lies behind these words slowly extinguishes certain habits from our daily life. For example, think about the heavy, massive radio receivers that existed back in the day. Over time, many of their buttons became viewed as "extra" and were removed, and with each reduction these devices eventually developed into the phones in our pockets. The scale of the object became smaller, and the functions of the buttons got lost in the three-dot menus and multilayered folders of our phones.

The list of examples like this one keeps growing every day, starting with Dieter Rams of Braun and continuing with Apple's Steve Jobs—as supposedly declining, obsolete, and dysfunctional items and their content reach more fruitful and productive forms with progress. These changes may seem harmless, but like the gray wolf from the Little Red Riding Hood—there may be more here than we realize at first glance.

Nowadays Mies van der Rohe's phrase "less is more" has seemingly unstoppable popularity. In part, it implies minimalism as a mindset, with its origins in Far Eastern cultures. The appreciation of natural beauty and simplicity begins there much earlier than European cultures, when Chan-Buddhism and Zen-Buddhism was formed in China and Japan under the influence of alterations of Mahayana-Buddhist and local lifestyle.

Instead of the icons and symbols found in Western traditions, expression focuses on simple stones, sand, and the immediate environment. This form of expression is implemented in such a manner that whatever remains is something that was already there: stone is left as stone, and sand is left as sand, without anything extra. This approach helps a human to develop a great ability to concentrate and protect the mind from distractions.

Western culture lagged behind the East, but its steps turned out to be radical and revolutionary in their own way. Each version of "less is more" obtained its own unique formation of artistic directions and disciplines; it now encompasses European directions rooted in the era of mass production and wild industrialization. In particular, it is worth noting twentieth-century modernist art and its main features, including antimimesis, dehumanization, formalistic emphasis, fragmentation, and chaos.

As authors and artists separated themselves from traditional genres and forms through a purposeful search for new methods, their work began to reflect this reality and yet not reject the old. Rather, adapting, altering, and continuing it differently, required simplification of objects and their content. Thus, modernism (and movements revolving around it, such as futurism, cubism, primitivism, fauvism, dadaism, purism, etc.) has always aimed to simplify the old or yet uninvented.

The inner freedom and unique mindset of modernists became a new form of expression in itself: one that does not reflect reality but rather creates it. And much like the Eastern, the object is left as the object and nothing else.

A final source for the current popularity of radical simplification is the era of uncontrolled mass production and technical reproducibility. This has penetrated works of art with a flick of a hand, just as water, gas, and electricity flow into our apartments. Under these conditions, anything that is massively and actively used requires a proper allocation of resources: this is always mastered by those who solve such complex tasks with the simplest formula.

Modernism in Design

The modernist era in graphic design began in Europe following World War I, influenced by art movements such as cubism, futurism, and de Stijl. The primary tools of expression in graphic design became bold typography, primary colors, simple geometric forms, and abstract compositions. In logo design, the goal was to simplify the form to its most functional appearance. Rational solutions were favored over the expressive, and universal appeal was valued over a culture-bound aesthetic.

The body of work created by modernists laid a solid foundation for modern logo designs. A certain language of form was invented, and there are certain elements that represent a fabric of modernist aesthetic. These include waves, stripes, stars, arrows, cubes, overlapping primitive shapes with exclusions, half and quarter circles, and spirals.

As we develop our skills as designers, it is important to observe modernist works and analyze the details. Think of the way we learn an alphabet and that allows us to write words; then knowing the meaning of the words allows us to express ideas. Likewise, in logo design knowing the visual language of modernists allows a designer to compose a design that has a solid foundation. Pay attention to elements such as structures, angles, composition, spacing between elements, and a correlation between positive and negative space. This practice will allow you to understand the system behind the logos and use some elements in your own design work with a fresh perspective.

Examples of the modernist aesthetic: simple geometric forms and repetition

Chapter 2
Types of Logo Designs

Pictorial Marks

Pictorial marks refer to logos that use a meaningful icon as a primary identifier of the brand. For example, the logos of Shell, Apple, Twitter, Target, and Starbucks are pictorial marks. They are by far the most widespread and effective forms of logo design.

Pictorial marks are powerful identifiers of the brand, and they directly or metaphorically represent the essence of the brand. If the brand wants to depict its activity via logo imagery, the most versatile form of expressing complex concepts would be via pictorial mark.

Pictorial marks have strong identifiability. For this reason they are usually accompanied by more neutral typography. This way the type does not overwhelm an already visually dense design and creates contrasts between the two. The end goal of a good pictorial mark is to be recognizable instantly without the brand's accompanying name.

Pictorial marks for various brands

Letterforms

A letterform is a type of glyph that represents an initial letter of the brand that conceptually, stylistically, or metaphorically depicts the brand's activity. For example, the logos of McDonald's, Airbnb, Tesla, Facebook, and Juventus are letterforms.

Most letterforms carry less visual information than pictorial marks and are simpler. Financial organizations and tech companies tend to favor letterforms over other types of logo design. While pictorial marks can have too much character, letterforms tend to be more neutral; therefore, they have a bit more timeless appeal.

Letterforms for various brands

Next page: *M* letterform

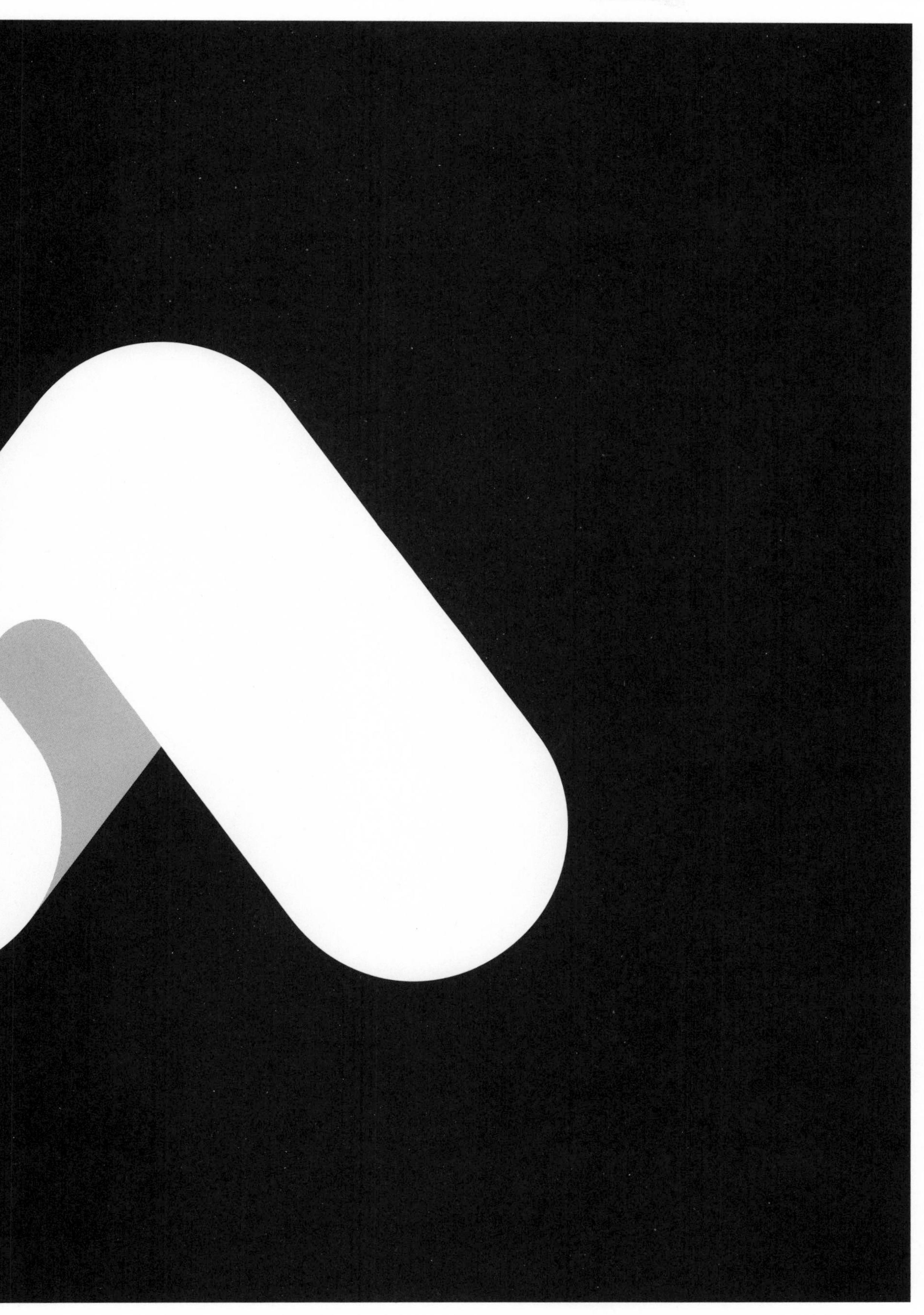

Abstract marks for various brands

Abstract Marks

Abstract marks are logos that represent an idea of the brand in a vague, subjective, suggestive manner. For example, the Nike, Adidas, Chase, Mitsubishi, and Microsoft logos are abstract marks.

Sometimes abstract marks are so abstract that certain arbitrary meanings are applied to them to connect with the brand's values. Typically, abstract logos do not represent any object in particular; rather, they are a depiction of a phenomenon. For example, in the case of Nike the intended association is speed.

Some phenomena, such as "connection," can be tied to strong visual ideas; others, such as "reliability," are hardly associated with any defined visual signs. In such cases, there is a need to give an arbitrary meaning to the mark. For example, the Chase logo represents the four parts of the octagon, representing forward motion; the white square in the middle originates from the center and suggests progress.

Wordmarks

Wordmarks (aka logotypes) are logos that depict the brand's identity solely using type. For example, the logos for FedEx, Google, Coca-Cola, and Disney are wordmarks.

For a wordmark to work well, the type needs to have a strong, defined character. It allows the mark to be distinct. If a neutral sans serif is used, then the involvement of some visual trickery, interesting ligatures, or incorporation of a certain sign in the type, as in the case of the FedEx logo, is necessary to make the wordmark memorable.

Sometimes the wordmarks are very clean in appearance. Certain types of minimalism create a very neutral, almost seamless, design aesthetic. This can be effective for B2B brands. If a brand wants to present a certain conceptual sophistication that differentiates them from the marketplace of overwhelming visual identities, then extreme minimalism is the way to go.

newwave

dreem

(Fo)RmuLa

Wordmarks for various brands

Next page: MARS logo modeled on NASA type

Monograms

Monograms are creative combinations of two or more initials of the brand. Nowadays, brands such as Hewlett-Packard, Louis Vuitton, Warner Bros., and Volkswagen use monograms as their logos.

Historically monograms appeared on coins representing the first two letters of the city name. Over time, monarchs also started to use monograms of their initials on the family insignias and other collateral materials. Today certain industries where a designer's name is the brand name favor using monograms; this is common in the fashion industry, for example.

Some letters have very interesting ways of interacting visually, but those with simple forms are hard to do as a monogram. The structure of *i* or *l*, for example, are not rich enough. By contrast, the more complex structure of a lower- or uppercase *s*, *w*, or *a* can usually be paired up with other complex letters to create interesting results.

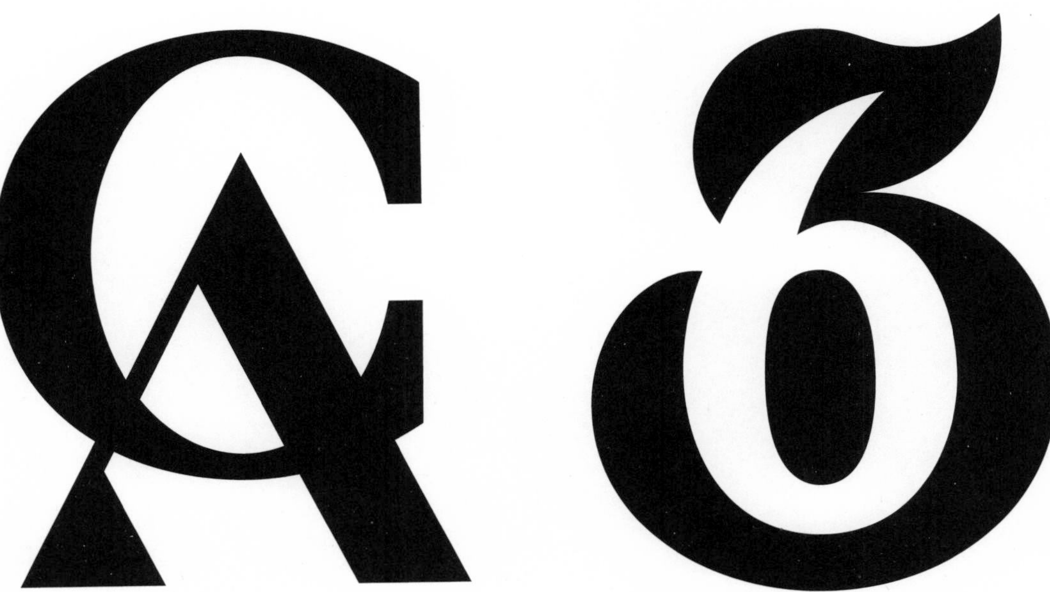

Monograms for various brands

Next page: Monogram for the International Association of Accessibility Professionals

Negative Space Marks

Every silhouette has a surrounding space. We refer to this as negative space. For a dark silhouette, bright space is considered negative; and, vice versa, for a bright silhouette the negative space is dark. Logos that utilize surrounding space as a part of a concept are called negative space marks.

Gestalt theory in psychology professes that an organized whole is more than the sum of its parts. That statement certainly holds true for negative space marks. When several conceptually distinct elements are combined in a unifying shape, utilizing negative space, the result is one of the most attractive and exciting logo designs.

A good negative space mark involves two or more strongly recognizable silhouettes harmoniously merged. One silhouette is positive and the other is negative. For example, when depicted from a frontal view, an apple has a very simple and distinct silhouette. By the sheer uniqueness of its silhouette, the apple is easily recognizable and cannot be mistaken for any other object. A simple leaf also has a distinct, simple silhouette. In simplified geometric terms, it is just two quarter circles connected.

Negative space logos are rare compared to other types, and they are arguably the hardest to create. A good result is possible only by cleverly combining two simple elements with distinct, easily recognizable silhouettes—and those two elements need to be conceptually related to each other.

Negative space marks for various brands

Logo system for Bellman (online news platform)

Logo System

In instances when a parent brand develops subsidiary brands, a logo system might be required to give each subbrand a distinct identity. Usually the symbol of the parent brand is used as a primary identifier; the subsidiary brands are distinguished by variation in color scheme or naming.

Developing logo systems is one of the most complex design tasks for a logo designer. It requires sound problem-solving skills and a strong sense of visual balance. In cases where the parent brand requires a more defined distinction, a specific visual language needs to be developed that creates a visual connection between the parent brand and the subsidiaries. Consistency of appearance and the repetition of the key visual elements are the primary principles for maintaining a unified look.

Pictograms

Pictograms are often described as part of a writing system: they are pictures that represent a word, expression, or idea. Each illustration operates as a universal symbol of the object it resembles or the concept it represents. A single pictogram or a consecutive group of pictograms are meant to be easily understandable by anyone, no matter what language they speak.

Pictograms have a degree of fluidity in how they are depicted. There is no single, specified version for each one, and they can be modified as needed. The slightest change in color, shape, and image does not make the pictogram meaningless. Sometimes, on the contrary, the changes enhance the meaning of the particular object, expression, or idea presented. Universality is a key factor of a pictogram design, and it is important to use the most primary of design elements (e.g., line, circle, square, triangle) as a base for more complex concepts.

Pictograms for Superhero; Online platform for influencers.

Cocreators: Nick Kumbari and Maria Akritidu

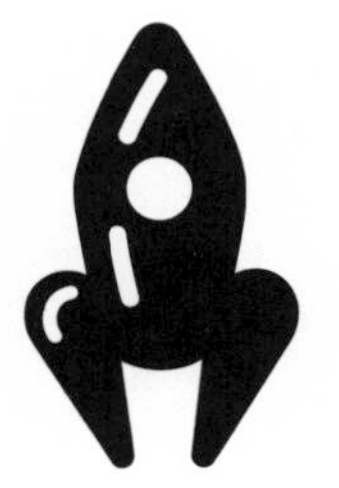

Patterns as Identity Elements

In many cases, our job is not just to design a company's logo—we create their branding. And perhaps the single most important part of this branding, after the logo itself, is producing a scalable pattern.

Patterns as part of brand identity usually need to complement the logo without duplicating it, and need to work printed on anything from a business card to an airplane, as well as parts of signage and interiors. The pattern is useful for anything that may require graphic treatments.

In these cases, specific patterns are developed so that the design requirements are met. Components of the brand marks can be used as a composing element of the patterns, and they usually yield good results because there is a visual connection between the mark and the pattern. When the brand mark does not have elements that can be readily turned into the pattern, it is necessary to develop a new visual language, either in contrast or on par with the brand.

Chapter 3
Visual Matters

Gradients

Gradients are beautiful effects that can take the edge off the piece and give it an ethereal look. In most cases, they are used as tools for shading (e.g., drop shadows) and for creating compositions involving multiple colors and transparencies.

Designers tend to use gradients frequently because they are effective and the gradient tool is easy to use. As a result, they have become ubiquitous and considered cliché. In logo design, there are practical concerns and aesthetic reasons to use gradients in moderation. In RGB some gradients might look stunning; when reproduced on paper, they lose vigor and vibrancy, especially when viewed on a smaller scale. Therefore, unless the logo will appear only on the web or some other digital platform, care must be taken to reduce the number of hues and ensure the RGB and the CMYK version will both be effective.

1.

2.

1. Owl mark for Studio George Bokhua

2. Logo proposal for NASA's In Space Manufacturing

Color Gradation Simplified

The fewer words a text contains, the easier it is to memorize. Similarly the less visual information the logo depicts, the more clear and memorable it becomes.

The gradient is a complicated graphic element, containing thousands of seamlessly merging hues. For some design purposes, color transitions with many colors are beneficial. For logo design, using a complex gradation often yields unclear and graphically overwhelming results. When the number of hues is reduced to a few instead of thousands, the result becomes much simpler and cleaner while maintaining the same effect. Also, when the piece is scaled down, the gradation between the color tones appears seamless, similar to the gradations with multiple hues. This approach not only simplifies the piece but yields visually favorable results.

Shade Gradation with Strokes

Creating tonal gradations with arrow-like strokes of various widths and length is a versatile method of expressing light and shading. It can be applied to a wide range of logo designs, and it works especially well on organic forms.

Engraving is one of the oldest forms of image making. Masters of etching and woodcutting used tools to carve out images on a hard surface; the shape of the tools determined the shape of the stroke. Usually the strokes took an arrow-like form, starting from a wide base and thinning down toward the tip. The highly controlled application of those strokes created very simple but realistic results. However, this extremely tedious process involved a careful, manual application of each stroke on a surface that was unforgiving of even minor mistakes.

Modern digital tools enable us to manually place each stroke at an appropriate spot and move it around. It's easy to change the width and length of the stroke, as well as the width and shape of the tip and the base. The versatility of application allows an untrained designer to organize and reorganize the strokes until the desired form is achieved.

When depicting complex human or animal characters, creating volume with strokes is often the most appropriate approach. It also works well on simple geometric shapes. Be prepared, though. Like engraving, it's still a tedious process, and it can take many hours to do it well.

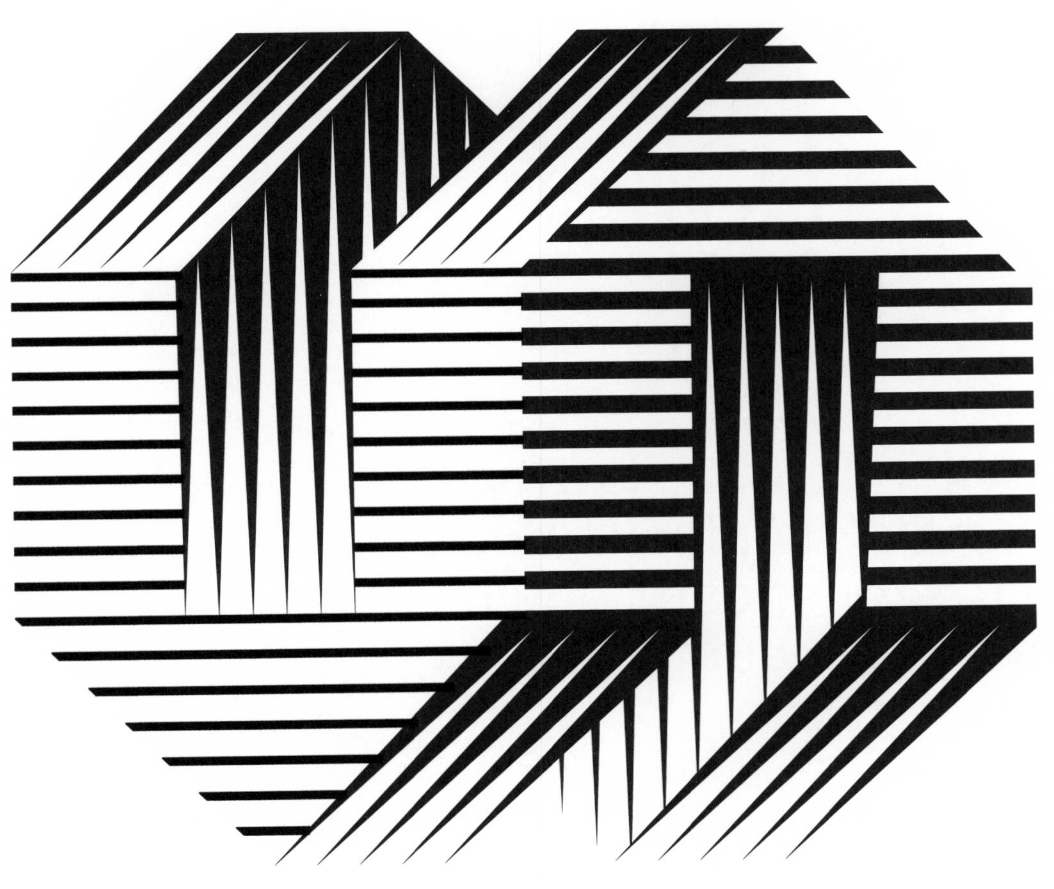

Light and Shading

1.

2.

Not everything simple is attractive: Simple marks can look sophisticated when they are made with proper care, and they can look plain if they lack content. There is a fine line between the two.

Simplicity has its charms only when it bears a certain amount of detail. Some shapes are too simple to be interesting. In cases where the mark looks plain, additional design elements are needed to bring it to life. Introducing a light source can do the trick. If it's applied correctly, the light adds depth and dimension to the mark. If a logo looks interesting in its most reduced state, introducing a light source is unnecessary. If its appearance is lacking, light and shading can save the piece from a mundane look.

Logo for Benson Seymour. (1) Without and (2) with introduced shading elements

Next page: bg by author

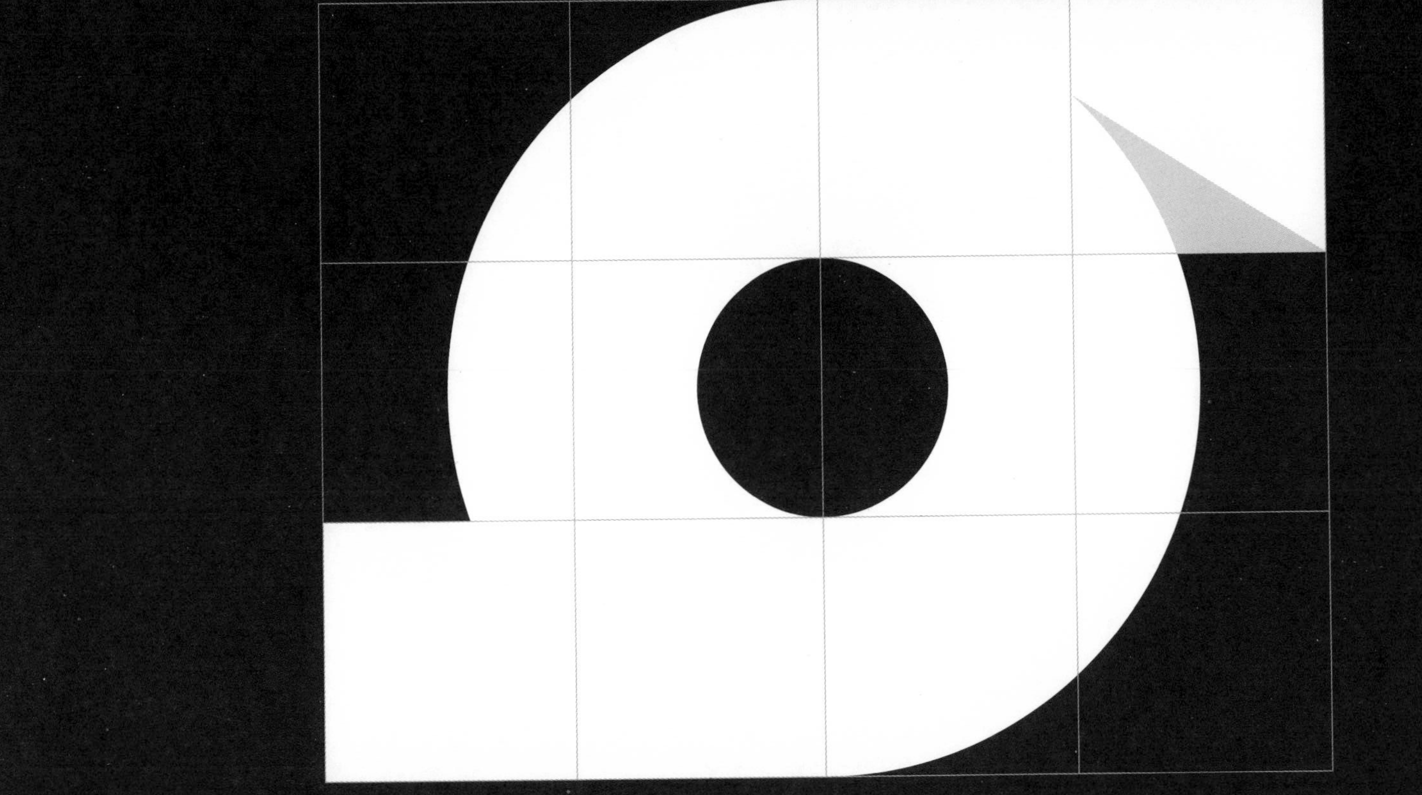

Shading of Hemisphere

The first exercise that most art schools do in the drawing class is the study of the hemisphere. This is because one of the most simple and omnipresent shapes in the universe has the smoothest and most multifaceted light shading features. The hemisphere has all points of its surface area equidistant from its core, allowing light to transition seamlessly to shadow. The six basic structural elements of light shading are highlight, midtone, reflected light, cast shadow, occlusion shadow, and core shadow.

It's beneficial for every designer to understand the light/shading structure of the hemisphere—it applies to various organic forms and geometric shapes. Logos lose sharpness and definition, when too many shades of gray are used. This is especially noticeable on a smaller scale. Note: An exception can sometimes be made when the silhouette of the mark is well defined. A strong silhouette makes the mark memorable regardless of the number of graphic elements it contains.

1. Highlight 2. Core shadow 3. Midtone
4. Reflected light 5. Cast shadow
6. Occlusion shadow

1.
2.
3.
4.
5.
6.

Light and Shading on Simple Marks

Letterform and abstract marks are usually simpler than pictorial marks; therefore, the shading needs to be more subtle. Usually it is best to use only one midtone. This way, the shading does not get in the way of other elements and the outcome is crisp.

Light naturally requires shading; but the appearance of a shadow implies that a light source is present. Provided that the designed mark has a strong silhouette, it is most appropriate to apply a gray shading on the elements that appear to lay or fold over other elements. This adds a sense of dimension to work, giving it depth and a level of sophistication.

R letterform. Skillshare tutorial

Chiaroscuro in Logo Design

The translation of the word *chiaroscuro* from Italian is "light-dark." It refers to a drawing technique that involves a reduction of mid-tones to achieve stronger contrasts. Renaissance artists widely used the technique; it allowed them to heighten the dramatic appearance of their paintings.

In logo design, the chiaroscuro technique is an expression of light and shading using only a few tones of gray or no mid-tone at all. Simplicity requires as little visual information as possible. In this case, using only a few tones yields a crisp, high-contrast outcome that is more visible and impactful.

To get a cleaner and sharper outcome, use fewer tonal variants when applying light shading to the piece. Highlight, shadow, a single mid-tone, and background color are usually enough to depict even the most complex figures.

George Bokhua. Self portrait.
Social media profile picture

Next page: Georgian Parliament

Logo Visibility

In a perfect scenario, a logo should look equally sharp on bright and dark backgrounds. Unfortunately, when the logo is designed for use on a bright background, it does not look good when inverted.

Most often, subjects that are bright in color require dark background, so the clear visibility of the shape is achieved. This does not pose the problem when the logo is expected to be used only on a colored background. Often the mark needs to look good on multicolored backgrounds, and sometimes inverting the color of the logo does the trick in these situations. Keep in mind that if you invert the color of the white swan, the result will be a black swan, and this may be the look you are searching for, or it may be undesirable. An element called a graphic device is required to aid the mark's visibility.

Crane mark

Graphic Device

A graphic device refers to a visual element that surrounds a logo to separate it from the background image.

The primary way to separate a logo from a background is to outline the silhouette of the mark with a sufficiently thick, bright stroke. This creates a border between the shape and the background, thus making it look more visible against dark or brighter backgrounds. The graphic device also allows the logo to look clear when applied to patterns, photos, or other visual materials.

When the logo is circular, the graphic device should be a circle. It goes well with the shape of the mark and in most cases yields the most pleasing results. For a logo with a lot of edges, the outcome still may not look pleasing no matter how smooth the outline of the graphic device is. In this case, using basic geometric shapes, such as squares or a circle, is advised.

Most of the printed and digital formats are rectangular in shape. The square graphic device fits well and is the safest and the most appropriate for these formats. Using basic geometric shapes as a graphic device might not yield the most aesthetic result, but functionally it works well.

IN SPACE
MANUFACTURING

IN SPACE
MANUFACTURING

ISM

Example 1 shows the VersaBank logo. The applied graphic device is a circle, rather than a triangle or a direct outline of the mark. This solution works well with the triangular mark since the negative space in relationship to circle/triangle appears balanced. If it was a square, the approach and result would differ. In this case the brand needed a device for the outdoor signage. The circular form is easy to reproduce and looks good as both projecting and frontal signage.

To the left: Bank of Georgia (Georgia)

To the right: VersaBank (Canada)

Black on White vs. White on Black

A white object on a dark background appears larger than the same-sized black object on a bright background. Galileo Galilei first discovered this visual illusion: Viewing with the naked eye, the planets appeared larger in comparison to the view through a telescope.

After examining how our brain responds to the visual stimulus, neuroscientists have discovered that dark stimuli create a more accurate representation of the object's actual size than light stimuli. This phenomenon is due to the way the brain interprets lightness versus darkness, and it is directly linked to the way we perceive color. Because of this irradiative effect of white color, black objects appear right-sized and white objects appear more exaggerated.

Black circle on white and white circle on black backgrounds, for comparison.

Same-sized Look

It's important for a logo to look the same size both on dark and bright backgrounds. Due to the natural inclination for bright objects to appear larger than dark ones of the same size, some adjustments must be made to balance the two.

The simplest technique is to simply scale down the bright mark. This quickly solves the problem and yields acceptable results. To achieve more sound results, shrink the mark: First, outline it with a stroke. Then the stroke must be expanded and subtracted from the shape area. Experiment with the width of the stroke until the final outcome, both black and white, appears visually similar. Note this in brand guidelines (see page 191), so the client is aware of where and how to use the correct logotype.

sensibill

Bone Effect

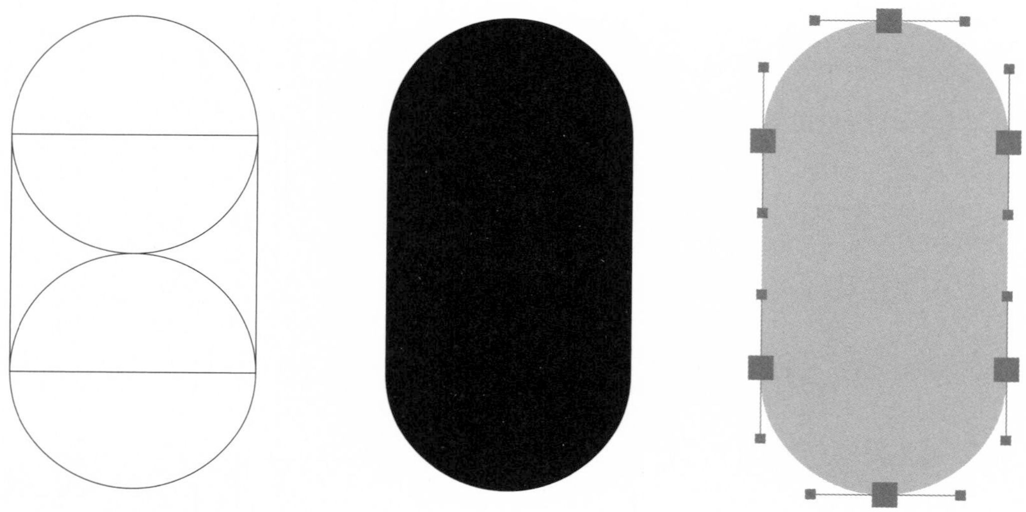

Where two circles meet a square, a peculiar visual paradox appears. This is called a bone effect: the sides of the shape look like they are indenting toward the center, resembling the humerus (the bone of the upper arm).

In typography, the bone effect appears most commonly in cases of the letter *O*.

Construction of the shape involving the bone effect.

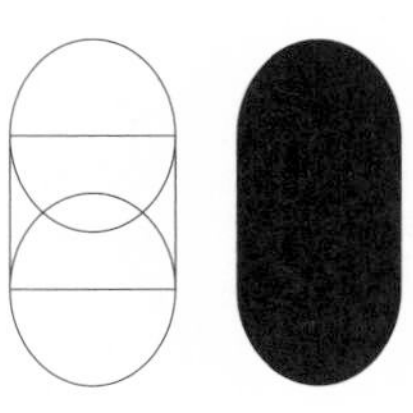

There are six anchor points in use. This solution creates a relatively smooth outcome but does not eliminate the bone effect.

The first technique consists of elongating the top and bottom circles into ellipses. This makes the connection between shapes less dramatic and creates a smoother transition. The technique is the quickest and simplest to apply. Unfortunately it does not completely solve the problem, and the bone effect is still a bit apparent.

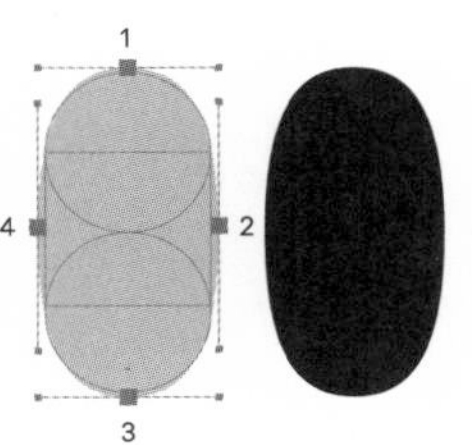

There are as few as four anchor points in use. This solution creates the smoothest outcome.

The second technique involves tweaking anchor points until the desired curve is achieved on anchors 1 and 2. Note that the reference shape is symmetrical in nature: To eliminate the bone effect the achieved curve can be copied and used as the remaining parts of the shape. Unfortunately the outcome of this technique is a bit exaggerated.

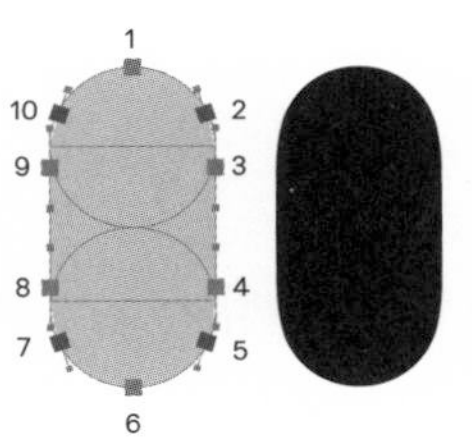

There are ten anchor points involved, yet a smooth outcome with the least exaggeration can be achieved.

The third technique involves ten anchor points. After the desired curve is achieved on anchors 1, 2, and 3, the curve can be copied and used for the remaining parts of the shape. This technique eliminates the bone effect and creates a smooth shape. Balancing three anchor points can be time-consuming, but it yields the most beautiful outcome.

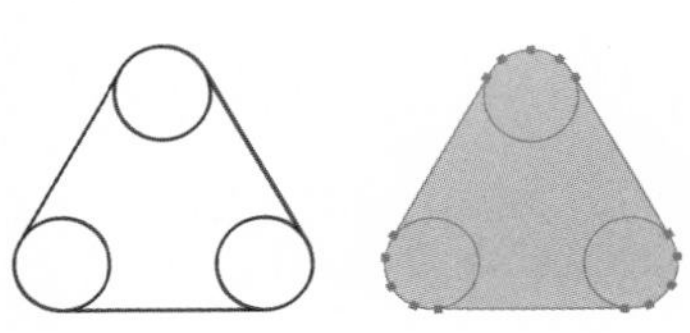

There are fifteen anchor points involved, yet a smooth outcome with the least exaggeration can be achieved.

The bone effect primarily appears when two circles connect with a rectangle, but similar visual phenomena can occur where three or more circles connect. In addition to the capsule shape, rounded triangles and rounded squares are the most common basic shapes with bone effects in their initial state. Only the application of technique number three can solve the problem.

Bone Effect in Logo Design

The visual illusion of indentation might take place in every case where a curve connects with a straight line. The amplitude of the curve reflects on how drastic the indentation will be.

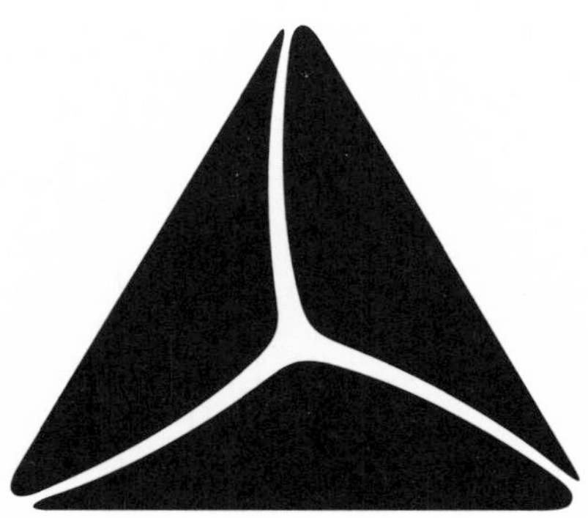

1.

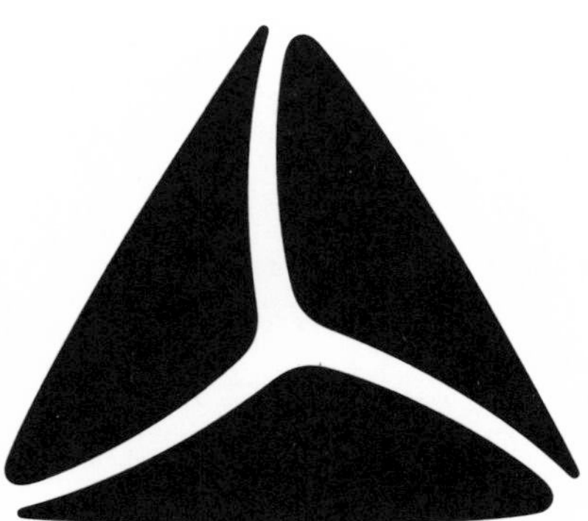

2.

In logo design, the bone effect appears quite frequently. Is it essential to fix every case? The answer is no. Sometimes fixing the shape negatively affects surrounding shapes, but there are instances where correcting the bone effect might be advantageous. For example, in the case of the negative space gorilla mark (example 2), the unfixed bone effect emphasizes the bulkiness of the front and back limbs of the gorilla. The effect was minimized on the left side of the head.

Example 1 depicts a logo of TBC Bank before the restyling and after. The client wanted the new logo to be more friendly and better suited for digital platforms. Fixing the bone effect made the mark look more rounded; it also helped free up the interior space making the logo look more crisp on a small scale.

TBC Bank; Logo before (1) and after (2) restyling

Negative space gorilla

Overshoot

Overshoot is an easy concept to overlook. Incorporating it in your designs can make a subtle but important difference.

The idea of overshoot was developed by typographers, who have been working with the same basic forms for centuries. They realized that rounded letters, such as *C* and *S*, give the illusion of being smaller than straight or angular letters, such as *M* and *T*, even if they are actually the same height. To adjust for this disparity, rounded letters should extend above and/or below the typical X-height of the typeface—they need to overshoot the standard limits.

Adjusting rounded forms to account for overshoot is best done in the final stages of design, when you have moved from paper to Illustrator and it's easier to make small changes (see Execution, page 163). Slight tweaks to an anchor point or two could make the difference between a great design and a perfect design.

Overshoot in logo design: connected triangle and circle

Next page: Overshoot in typography

Next page after: Overshoot in logo design: 236 mark

K letterform for Keikkatiimi (manufacturing industry). A concept demonstrates incorporation of an electric thunder bolt with the letter *K*

Balancing

Balancing refers to a process where the smallest parts of the logo are adjusted to achieve balance. Every logo design task is unique, and it is virtually impossible to generalize the ways in which a mark can be balanced. Here are a few general concepts that can be applied to most logos.

1. Stability: The logo should not feel unnecessarily tilted to the right or left. The sense of gravity and balance must be present. If the concept allows, the base of the mark should be heavier; a wider base will appear more firm and grounded.

2. Proportion: The overall proportions of the logo should aim to be a square rather than a rectangle. If a symbol is too long or too wide, it becomes inconvenient to use. Also the squared proportion is more favorable for type lockup than rectangular.

3. Composition: Elements within a logo design should be more or less equally spaced. It creates visual dissonance if elements are clustered in one part of the logo and free in another.

4. Consistency: Boldness or the thickness of the elements should be relatively similar. Having very thick and very thin elements within the piece creates a sense of imbalance. Also, if the logo is made with a stroke, the width of the stroke should be consistent throughout.

5. Scalability: The logo must look good and clear when enlarged or scaled down.

Visual Paradoxes

A definition of a paradox is a seemingly absurd or contradictory statement or proposition which, when investigated, may prove to be well-founded or true. The same applies in the visual world. If something appears as one thing but changes upon further examination, a curious visual phenomenon takes place where the mind engages in a problem-solving activity—and discovering a solution brings a sense of joys.

Some techniques can be employed to make a seemingly mundane shape into something more interesting. Experimenting with layers, interlacing shapes, shading, juxtaposing dimensions, and playing with colors are tools that can improve a logo and make it more memorable.

Flip Casa. Real estate

Next page: Relative numbers (experimental work)

Types of Visual Paradoxes

There are three distinct types of visual paradoxes, but they all create certain visual effects that somewhat challenge the nature of reality.

1. Impossible figures: Forms that are designed in a way that cannot exist in the real world.

2. Ambiguous forms: Images where an object looks like one thing but turns into something different upon further investigation.

3. Illusions of motion: Compositions where a clever arrangement of certain shapes causes still images to appear moving or animated.

There are cases where the paradoxes intermingle, and there are cases where the illusion cannot be categorized.

Composition of numbers 1 to 9
(experimental work)

Impossible Figures

When a 2-D shape in some parts appears 3-D, or when a 3-D shape is designed in a way that will not be plausible if it was real, this creates the optical illusion referred to as an "impossible figure."

The Penrose triangle, created by Swedish artist Oscar Reutersvärd, is one of the most elegant examples of the impossible figure. At first glance, the figure looks sound, but after further examination, the plausibility of the figure becomes questionable. Mathematician Roger Penrose popularized the shape and called it "impossibility in its purest form." The irrational cube created by M. C. Escher is also a very good example where a seemingly 3-D form in some parts looks 2-D.

(1) Penrose triangle (2) Escher's cube

1.

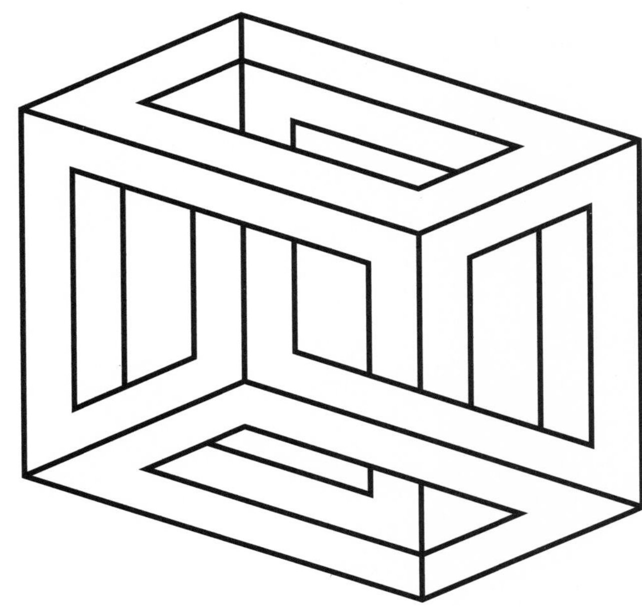

2.

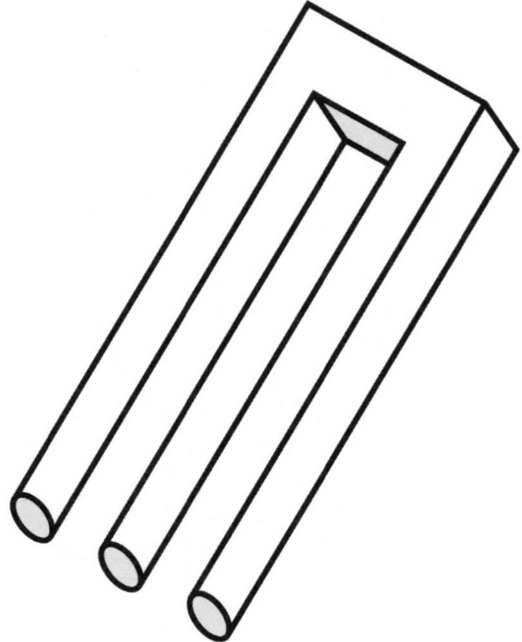

1.

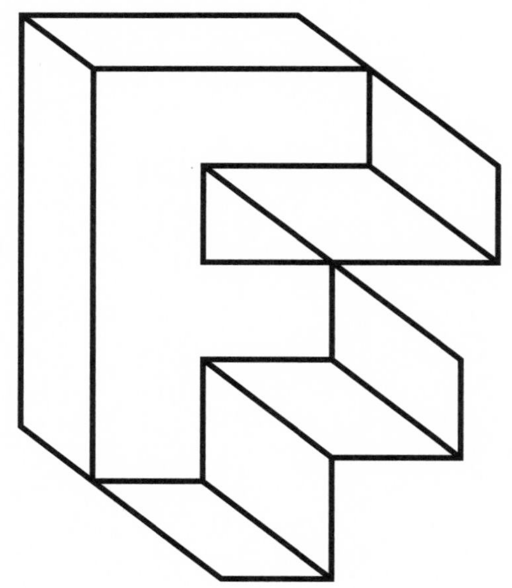

2.

(1) Blivet fork (2) *F* letterform

Next page: Nebo (film production)

Impossible Figures and Logo Design

Reversing perspectives, manipulating line connection, and misaligning layers can create visual effects that challenge metaphysical truths. The designer should carefully study the concepts of prominent artists who are known for creating optical illusions. This opens your mind to possibilities in the field and suggests existing principles and techniques that can be modified and creatively applied to your designs.

This example demonstrates how a concept (to the left) behind the impossible trident (also known as blivet or devil's tuning fork) was applied to the *F* letterform without directly copying the solution. The bottom part of the blivet suggests that toward the top, the shape should continue as a three-part cylinder; instead the cylinders turn into a cubic form of two connected composing parts. In the case of the *F* letterform, the bottom right part suggests that the perspective should remain the same moving toward the top, but it changes at a certain point and moves toward a separate direction.

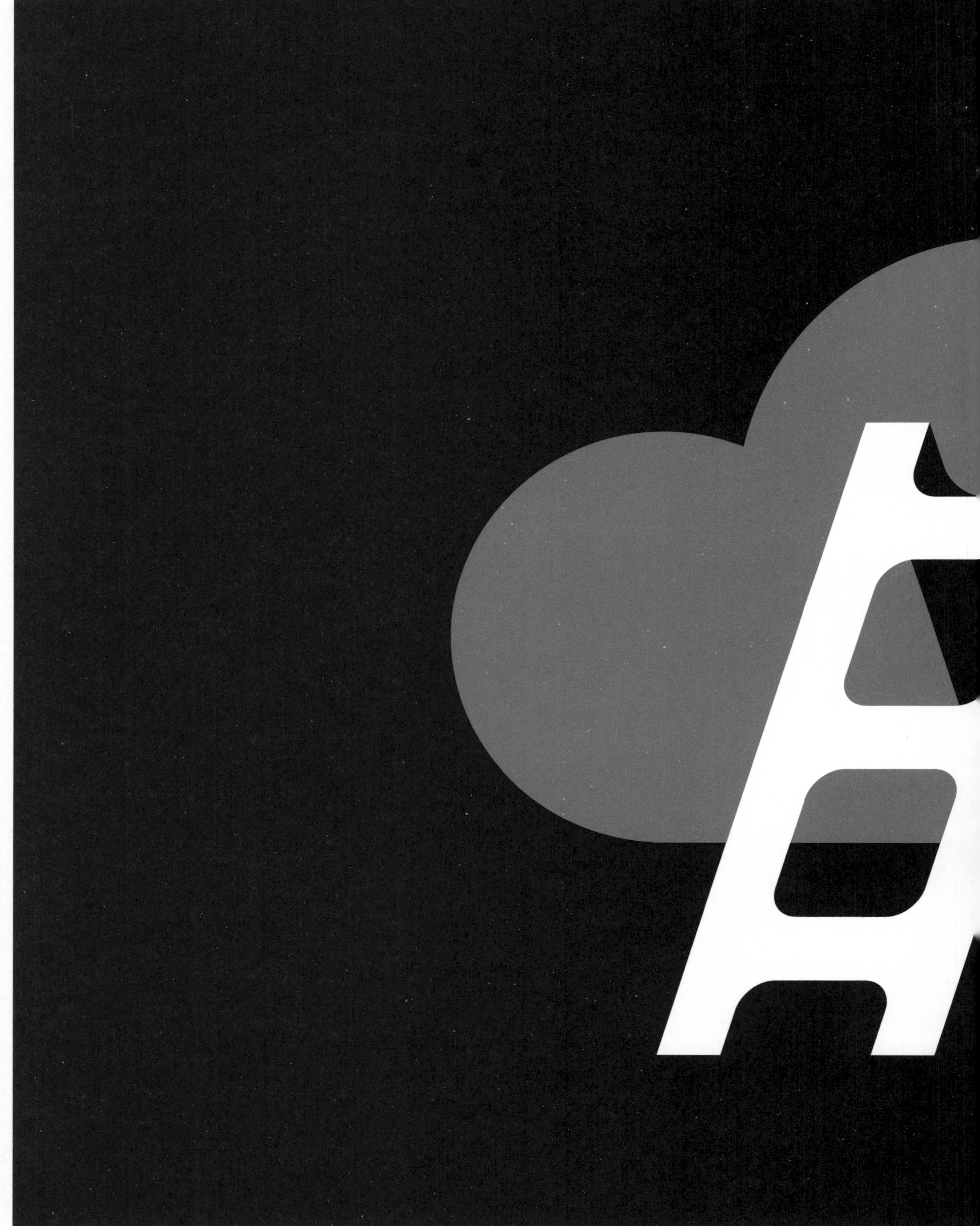

Motion Illusion

During the Industrial Revolution, the creation of film allowed artists to see motion in a new way, spurring an art movement called futurism. The movement concentrated on a depiction of speed, dynamism, and motion in form. *Dynamism of a Dog on a Leash*, painted by Giacomo Balla in 1912, is a classic example of a technique expressing a movement.

There are various ways that speed can be expressed. One of the simplest ways is a swoosh, like the Nike logo. A more complex exam-ples is a former Formula 1 logo. These two examples carry a specific correlation; they both depict motion via an arrow-like dynamic that starts from a thin point enlarging at the end.

When depicting speed, it is advisable to have the thinner part start-ing from the left increasing in volume to the right; the logo will read better because it follows the direction of reading text in Western cultures. There are few other methods of depicting motion, and any pattern or element that increases from a shallow composition into a more dense one creates a subtle motion.

Rotating Earth symbol with lines representing speed and data units; Proposal for PepsiCo data analytics

Ambiguous Forms

Ambiguous forms are not a common occurrence in logo design, and there are very few successful cases in use. It is important to notice them when they arise though, because they may appear unintentionally and are often sexual in nature.

When a designer is fully involved in the process for a prolonged time, the graphic elements that you are working on become overly familiar and your brain gets used to perceiving the objects in a certain way. When this occurs it's sometimes almost impossible to see beyond that preconceived representation, even when you take a rest and view the work with fresh eyes. Given this, it is important to keep in mind how easy it can be for a designer to fail to notice elements of their piece that are quite obvious to others who view it.

This tendency is something to be aware of on any project. When a design that is sexual in nature is made intentionally and in accordance with the concept, then everything is dandy. But if unintended sexual connotations appear in a designer's work, it may go unnoticed by the designer, the client, or even by everyone involved with the project. There have been notorious cases when even clients failed to notice the sexual connotations, and the logos went public. This can break the brand, so proper care must be taken to avoid such mishaps.

Negative space elephants often confused with a whale symbol

Symmetry vs. Asymmetry

Perfect symmetry does not exist, and you must beware of designing perfectly symmetrical logos. Aiming for perfect symmetry, as beautiful as it sounds, oftentimes yields boring design outcomes.

A certain degree of asymmetry within the mark can help to keep the viewer interested and engaged with the composition. This is frequently the case when the silhouette appears symmetrical. Variations and combinations of multiple elements bring energy to the work, while repetitions due to mirroring or copying design parts appear boring.

The feeling of asymmetry can be achieved in a subtle way by simply changing a color, adding and subtracting minor details, or mirroring and offsetting parts. The end goal is to develop a visual that keeps eyeballs traveling, creating excitement and fresh stimulus throughout the composition.

Black and white swans (experimental work)

Cat marks; Solid and line versions
(experimental work)

Solid vs. Line

Solid logos have a stable, strong appearance. On the other hand, logos made out of lines are light and elegant. A designer must be careful to choose the approach that is appropriate for the project. Some designs appear effectively in line and in solid shapes. When this occurs, the brand should select one approach as the primary and the other as secondary.

Solid icons have stronger appearance. When scaled down, the silhouette is clear and the concept is visible. They are more visible from far distances, provided that silhouette is well defined. The boldness also makes these icons show up well across various mediums.

The elegant look of a line design creates a seamless appearance due to its lightness. This is very useful in cases where a passive design approach is required. In cases of UI iconography (e.g., web and app icons) and interior signage, designs created with lines communicate their purpose without being overwhelming. The downside is that lines are not too visible from far distances. When scaled, these logos will have a weaker, more transient appearance, unless the width of the strokes is sufficient to stand out.

Cat one-liner (experimental work)

Griffin symbol; mascot for the Brazilian Jiu-Jitsu Club

Powerlifter icon (experimental work)

Sharp vs. Round

Logos with sharp shapes appear more threatening and authoritarian. Rounded shapes make symbols look inviting and friendly.

Sharp, edgy objects made of hard material have the potential to harm us: if enough force is applied, they have a natural ability to cut and penetrate things. As humans, our internal knowledge of this tends to make us more careful around such objects as knives, needles, razors, etc. Even though an image of a knife poses no danger, when we look at it, we still feel subconsciously that minor caution is needed.

By contrast, rounded objects seem to invite us to touch them. Objects with spherical shapes such as a cup, a remote control, a baseball, or a steering wheel propose no threat; therefore, they are more inviting to hold.

In logo design, keep these responses in mind when considering the task at hand. A designer must try not to use too many sharp elements, at least in the silhouette of the mark, unless it is appropriate to the project. Whenever possible, rounded shapes are preferable simply because they appear more friendly. After all, isn't almost every brand trying to appear friendly and inviting?

Jumping fox; Skillshare online tutorial

Pattern as a Design Element

At the heart of a good pattern is its grid. Square grids provide the most versatility, as they are more scalable and more adaptable; but they are also the most frequently used, leading to a sense of sameness among different brands. Instead experiment with different basic shapes, such as triangles.

The older identity of the City of Rotterdam uses hexagons to stunning effect in their branding, creating distinctive and recognizable, almost pixelated images using the shape. Another option is to try slightly different approaches to common shapes, such as rotating a square by 45 degrees to create a diamond.

A tessellation is a repetition of similarly shaped forms. If you have a tessellated pattern, color variations or variations within the tessellated units can create interesting patterns. Tessellations can be a relatively straightforward solution to the question of pattern, but the repetition quickly becomes boring. It's best to avoid tessellations in favor of a grid that lends itself to more variety.

Though it is secondary to the grid, color is another key consideration when working with patterns: Color distribution must be even and balanced. Too much color contrast can disrupt the flow of the pattern and distract viewers. Too little can lead to the design being overlooked—a failure when brand recognition is the goal.

Creating an effective combination of pattern and color can be difficult. Seeing how the pattern will re-create and repeat at these

Pattern design (work in progress)

Next page: 1932 mark (experimental work)

different scales is a quick way to determine the overall effect. It can be helpful to both the designer and client to create mock-ups of the pattern in use in practical situations. Be sure to use a variety of sizes, such as on a letterhead or on a wall in an office.

If the client intends to use the pattern for print purposes, such as marketing materials, be mindful of the CMYK balance and how the printing process works. As each of the four basic colors is printed individually, heavy use of complex colors can create a page that is literally oversaturated with ink. Using more basic colors means the paper will be better able to dry between color applications, giving you a sharper, cleaner look. It is always essential to closely examine printed proofs before approving any printing project.

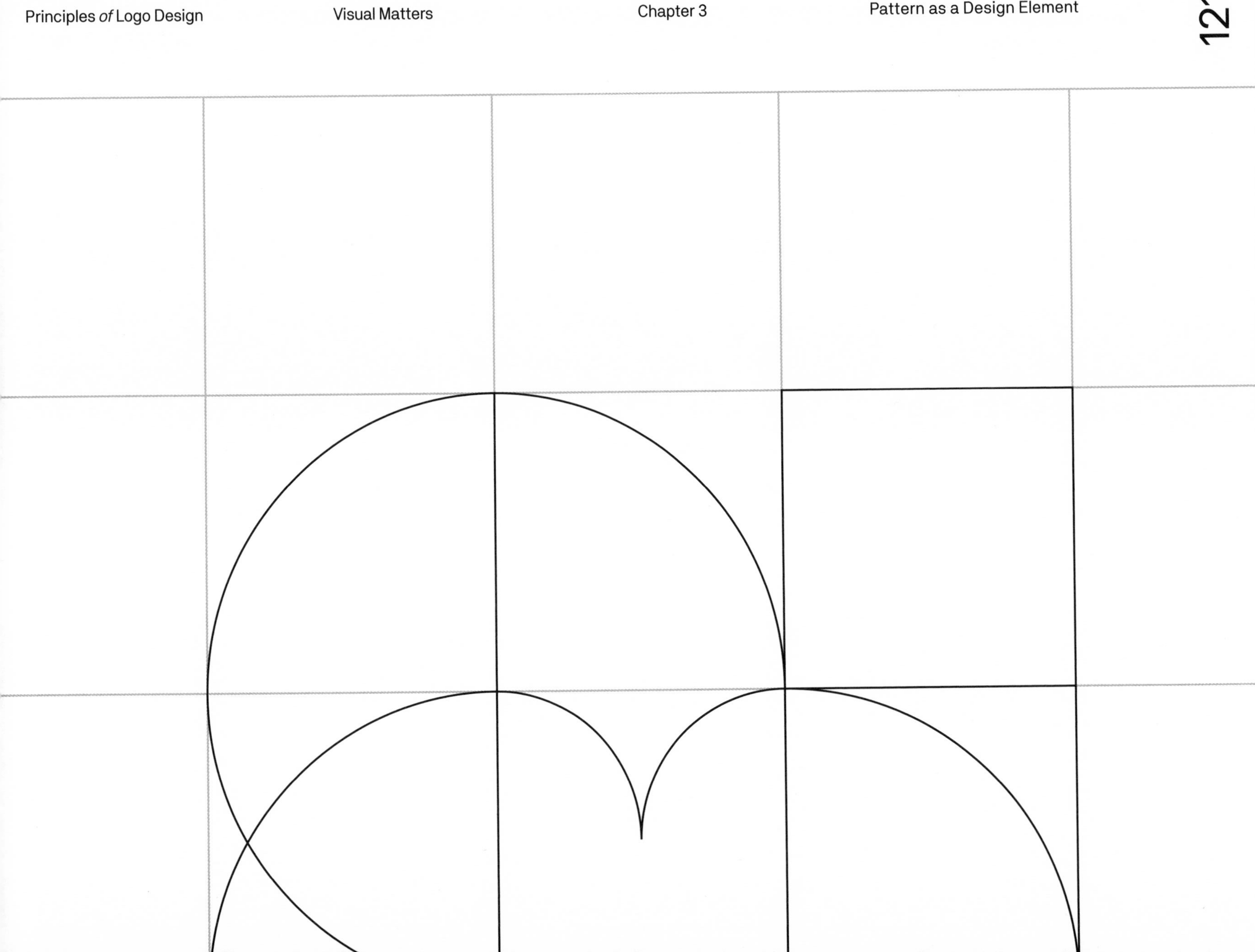

Dimension

The development of 3-D technologies introduced new inspiration to graphic design. Realistic 3-D designs tend to have too many details to work well as logos. But when the dimension is achieved by the simplest means, it can be very attractive.

Modernists mostly favored flat, 2-D shapes. This was due to utilitarian factors and to some extent a lack of tools to visualize complex 3-D shapes. Flat, simple geometric forms are limited in their range of variation. As a simple analogy, there are a limited number of ways to combine a square and a circle that will produce a result that looks interesting. In logo design, when all the possible variations are used, then logos start to look similar. Adding a dimension to logo designs brings a wider range of possibilities and increases the variety of original outcomes.

F letterform. Proposal for the Fandom. Online fan club

Dialectical Approach

The dialectical approach refers to a technique where two solutions are put side by side and compared in order to select the favorable one.

A refined sketch rarely reaches the level where it can be called final. After the refined sketch is imported to the digital platform, the piece is traced using the pen tool. Then usually some tweaking and additional solutions are needed to bring the design closer to what will be the final look.

Some solutions are deceptive: they look appropriate in the moment, but they don't hold up upon later examination and review. Sometimes this can be because of overexcitement on the designer's part. It's easy to be captivated by the novel appearance of a change that was made. Other times it is because of the inability of a designer to foresee all of the possibilities—the subsequent potential solutions and how compatible they may be with the current one.

A dog icon (experimental work)

Next page: experiments with the letter *M*

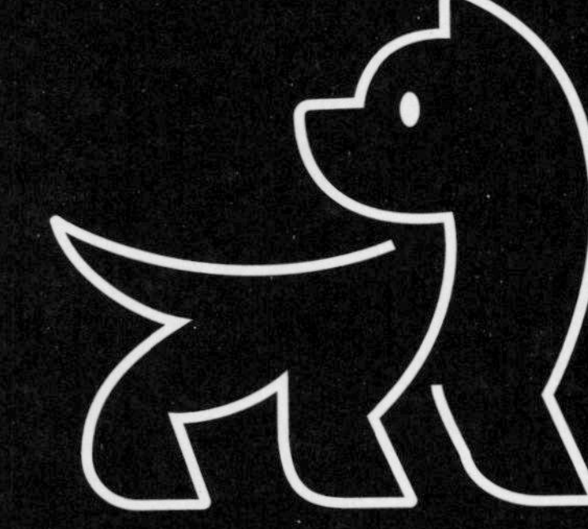

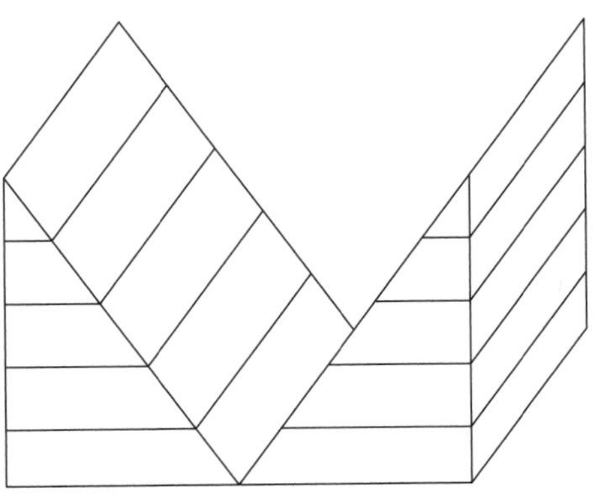

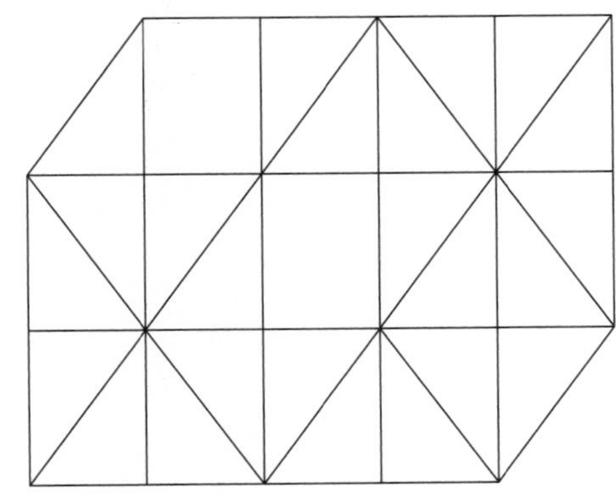

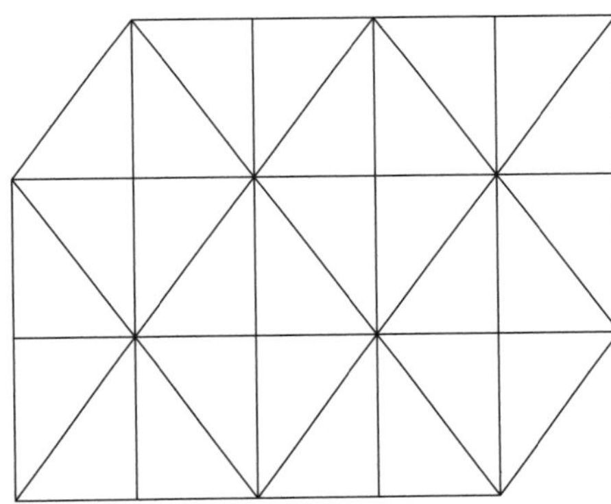

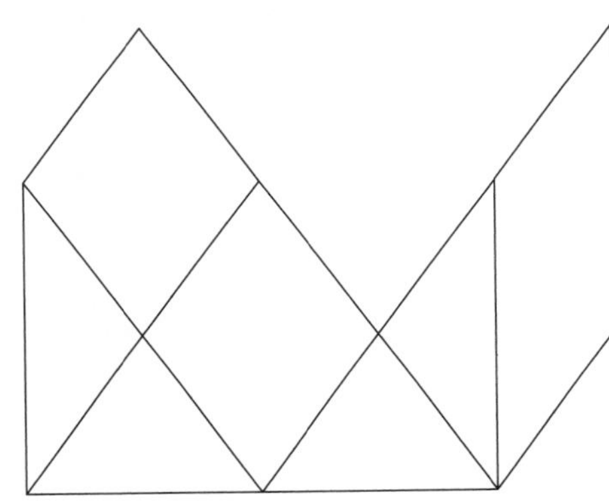

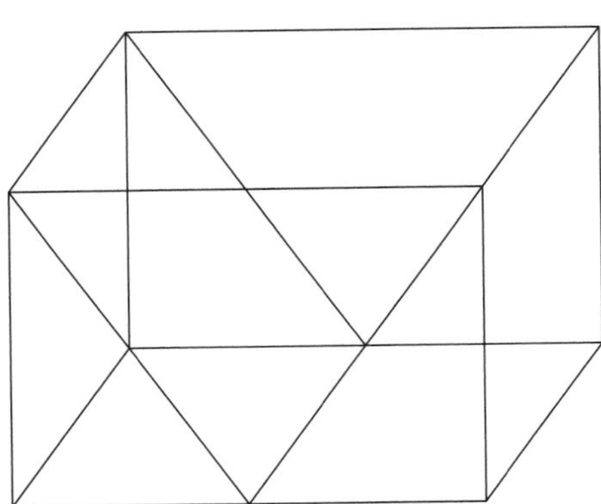

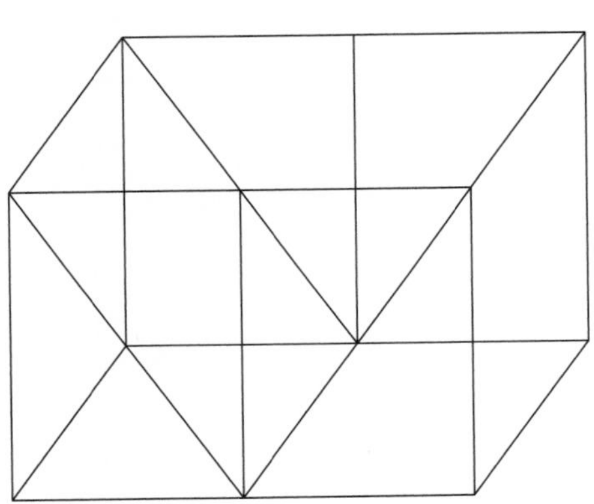

Suppose a designer works on a logo, constantly changing elements in the search for a better solution. In the process, some lesser solutions get favored and correct ones get overlooked. To avoid this, be sure to take simple precautions. Copy the work at each moment a new solution is discovered. Afterward, place the solutions next to each other, carefully examine and compare them, and select the one that best suits the project.

Copying work at each stage of logo design also allows a designer to return and work on some earlier solutions. This is especially helpful if the one that you selected initially did not develop into the result you were seeking.

When tasting different foods, we need a palate cleanser to help us get a better taste of subsequent foods. When designing, there are a few ways to rest your eyes, cleanse your visual palate, and make more objective decisions. When several solutions have been created, place the logos next to one another. Before a decision is made on which one to continue with, take a rest. When a designer is continually involved in the design process for hours, the decision-making becomes less objective due to fatigue. Taking some time off and looking at the design with rested eyes allows you to notice things that were not noticeable before.

Another method that is useful when reviewing a mark with complex features is to view the piece's mirror image. When the eye gets used to the design, seeing it in a mirrored state allows you to get a fresh perspective. Some portrait painters employed a similar technique: An actual mirror was placed next to a portrait to reveal the defects of the work and allow an artist to make adjustments. When viewing the logo in a mirrored state, some inconsistencies in proportions become clear. This change in perspective is especially helpful when designing animals or human characters.

Supahero; Social media for the influencers
(work in progress)

ANDREW HOWARD WORKSHOP AT THE STAMBA

WHAT:
EDITORIAL
DESIGN
WORKSHOP

WHEN:
SEPTEMBER
14,15,16

WHO:
ANDREW
HOWARD FROM
THE
ANDREW
HOWARD STUDIO

WHERE:
STAMBA
HOTEL,
4 MERAB
KOSTAVA ST,
TBILISI

HOW MANY:
ONLY
TWENTY
SPOTS

HOW MUCH:
ONLY
TWO
HUNDRED
DOLLARS

Project#2

PROJECT#2 IS A NON PROFIT EVENT INITIATED BY GIA BOKHUA AND GIORGI POPIASHVILI IN ASSOCIATION WITH THE STAMBA HOTEL. IT AIMS TO INSPIRE DESIGN PROFESSIONALS [illegible] IMPROVE THEIR SCILLS IN TYPOGRAPHY AND EDITORIAL DESIGN

Composition

When composing design elements, we seek to create something interesting that keeps a viewer engaged and connected. As designers we sense that we can arrange line, shape, color, texture, and space to create an infinite number of possible outcomes. But which arrangement is right? There is no set of hard-and-fast rules to give us practical guidance. Mostly this is learned by subjective judgments and trial and error.

A good composition is an artistic arrangement of elements that has a certain order (or disorder) that corresponds in some respects to physical reality. First define the goal of composition: What does the design need to express? Harmony, tension, dynamics, balance, dissonance, entropy, etc.?

With a goal in mind, a designer must pay attention to how the shapes behave when they interact with each other. For example, if we place the same-sized circle on top of a square, the composition will have a sense of harmony. If we reverse the sequence and put a square on top of the circle, there will be a sense of tension in the composition. If we place a circle next to the top of a triangle, a sense of motion will be apparent. And if we put a circle right on top of the triangle, a certain sense of balanced and tension is achieved.

Those are all subjective judgments. But years of playing with forms gives a designer an understanding and feel for the dynamics between the forms—this becomes a natural part of your arsenal.

Poster for the Andrew Howard workshop

Clock design with experimental numbers

Next page: Logo for the ACT research center;
Created by a chain of accidents

Experimentation and Accidents

Experiments and accidents are where the true magic of design happens. When you're not bound by a brief and a client's desires, you're free to relax and allow the design process to be fun. Creating works that are the opposite of what you are used to (or what you enjoy) is a practice that grants you freedom from yourself and allows you to venture into new territories and explorations.

Experimentation is essential for a designer's development, and it cannot be stressed enough just how important this is. When experimenting, a designer is not limited to one medium. Sketching, painting, sculpting, folding paper, anything works if the aim is to make something that is outside your comfort zone. If a designer works only in black and white, then bold, toxic colors are a welcome experiment. If a designer is good with solid marks, experiments with lines must be made. If your practice is clean and simple, then messy, rough work must be tried.

This is not work to present to a client; nor is it advised to make such work public. It should be done for the sole reason of freeing yourself from yourself for a brief period of time in order to find new design solutions—and perhaps run into lucky accidents.

We become designers because we enjoy the creative process, and when you're feeling stressed or burnt out, doodling or sketching can help you recharge by giving you the courage to be creative and reminding you of that joy. Allow yourself to do something dirty or ugly. Leave your comfort zone and explore different styles, textures, grids, or colors. The end result may be something you would never show your dog, let alone a paying client, but there may be something you discover in that process that will inspire future work. Forcing yourself out of your comfort zone can get you out of a rut and help you grow as a designer.

Look for inspiration in your daily life—the shapes your dog's body makes as they run, the suggested image in a cloud. Find those shapes that snag your interest and play with them. When something catches your eye, there's usually a reason.

And those times when your pencil slips or your cat spills coffee on your sketchbook? What may first seem like a setback or even a disaster could be exactly what your project was missing. Take a moment to look at your accident as an opportunity and see where it might lead you. There's no set definition of what is beautiful or good, so you never know what is going to work.

Letter *R* combination with the Rolling Stones' tongue

Next page: Experimental composition with strokes

ellensara®

Copying vs. Imitation

Copying work is something that frequently comes up in the design world, and there is a fine line between imitation and unethical use of someone else's intellectual property. With access to the internet and copy/paste keys, the ease and temptation of copying another person's design is higher now than ever. It can be difficult to keep your artistic integrity, but passing off light modifications to an existing work as your own original creation is damaging to all involved.

As designers, we are surrounded by countless examples of logos that can become valid sources of inspiration. Logos are effective because they make an impression on a viewer's mind, and logos we have seen in the past may be forgotten in our conscious mind but are still present. Likewise, there may be cases where a forgotten visual solution reappears to us as we work and we take it as our own solution.

S letterform for a company that manufactures beauty products

The best way to avoid this is a simple rule of thumb: If a solution feels familiar even in a slightest manner and it is not yours, then it is definitely someone else's. It needs to be disregarded or modified significantly.

When modernists first began creating logos, they used basic shapes: squares, circles, triangles. These basic shapes remain an integral part of logo design today. Almost all inspiration can be taken from these very first designs. When you find yourself drawing inspiration from some of these basics, push further and find your own new solution. Tweak enough of the reference to make it your own. Advancements in modern technologies can aid us in modifying those basic shapes. After all, modernists were designing by hand without the luxury of quickly copying elements, easily fixing anchor points, or having 3-D options and other current tools.

Sometimes we don't realize we are copying (or nearly copying) another designer's work. If this happens, be honest and humble. If the work gets accepted by the client, then contact the original artist, let them know what happened, and offer them compensation. Likewise, if someone has copied your work, contact that designer first to discuss the situation. If you don't find their response acceptable, there are legal avenues you can explore. Also most online platforms are very competent in assessing copyright infringement. The work will be taken down if you have a reasonable proof, and in extreme cases the artist can be banned.

Client Relations

Client relations are very important for the design process, and the more friendly and collaborative the atmosphere, the better the outcome. It is important to remember that any feedback, even the kind you do not like, is valuable. Also keep in mind that some clients, due to the lack of experience, have seemingly unreasonable demands that the designer should accommodate to the best of their ability without losing their soul.

One of the most common mistakes I have seen beginners make is not valuing feedback from clients. It is easy for it to feel like criticism or an attack on your work or integrity. Try not to be too in love with your creations—at the end of the day, the designs are for your client as well as for yourself. Most of the time, clients have clearer understanding of the brand they are developing so listening to them is crucial to success as well as being hired again or recommended to others.

Another common mistake made by beginners and the most advanced of designers alike is demonizing clients. While client requests may seem irrational, tedious, or confusing, it is key to remember that their goal is not to hurt your feelings. While constructive criticism can be subjective, it is possible to find something constructive in any criticism you get.

Real-life Objects as Aids

A designer must not shy away from using real-life objects as an aid. If the concept is hard to visualize due to the complexity of its form, these objects can make the design process easier and even point you in new directions.

Sketching complex figures without a reference is very hard unless you possess a talent for it. Even when a figure is clearly conceived in your mind, sometimes it is helpful to have a 3-D mock-up of the concept. This allows a designer to view the object from various angles and perhaps discover a more interesting viewpoint or a solution.

Plasteline, adhesive tape, metal wire, paper, wood, a 3-D printer, a laser cutter—these can all come in handy to create a figure that can be physically manipulated. Real objects can be observed and interacted with in a manner that acquaints a designer with its formal details. Mistakes and inconsistencies also become more apparent.

Clock design with experimental numbers;
laser-cut prototype, plywood

Chapter 4
Design Process

Concepting

Logos are identifiers of the brands that conceptually, stylistically, or metaphorically reflect the essence of the brand. Marks that depict clever concepts and have sound, visual appeal make the strongest first impression and, in general, are more effective.

Finding the right concept for the brand is not a simple task. It needs to be clever and visually pleasing. As you begin the process, it's essential to have a name and a detailed design brief. Information, starting from the brand's big idea to the minuscule details on how they plan to operate, will become handy as you design.

(Top left) The central part of the mark represents a paper, a bill in particular. (Top right) The top and the bottom parts of the mark are continuations of the central part. (Bottom right) The top and the bottom parts are cropped to achieve the shape of letter *S*. (Bottom left) The final shape is refined so it looks smooth yet sharp.

Logo for the Georgian Pediatric Association

In the brief, it's important to have down-to-earth, rational, and clear design directions. Stating basic characteristics, brand persona, demographic segment, competitors, and desired color scheme is sometimes not enough. Often the most important clues are adjectives that reflect the idea of the brand are some of the most useful for the design process. Such adjectives give abstract visual clues that can aid in the concepting process and be made into meaningful symbols.

Beware of the brief that gives complete creative freedom; usually, it is a sign that the client does not have a vision of the brand and expects a designer to provide the vision. This can be achieved *if* dozens of initial concepts and iterations are expected, but usually there are not enough to provide a correct solution. There are cases when creative freedom works the designer's favor, but unfortunately most often it works against you.

It's preferable for a designer and a client to communicate their ideas about how they think their brand should look, at least stylistically. Some logo references from your own portfolio and works of other designers can become very helpful as reference material and ensure that expectations are well defined and can be met.

For the design brief, a designer must also ask about the brand personality and demographics (e.g., age, gender, nationality). This information helps when deciding the overall aesthetic of the brand. Concepts designed for children, for example, tend to have a more colorful, rounded, friendly look. Concepts designed for female products have a tendency toward the natural. The aesthetic of brands with male characteristics leans toward boldness. Concepts designed for different cultures may include symbolic elements that reflect ethnic or national characteristics.

That said, the brand personality does not necessarily need to be aligned with the targeted demographic audience. For example, some identities designed for the Asian audience have a European aesthetic; some male-oriented brands can have a feminine look; and even some children products can have identities that appeal to adults. This all depends on a brand strategy, a document that provides information about the brand's big idea, and a long-term development strategy.

In ideal cases, the design brief is accompanied by the brand strategy, but unfortunately, not all brands can afford a fully developed strategy in their early stages. (This is especially worth noting because most brands that need logos are start-ups.) To make things even more complicated, sometimes neither naming of the brand nor the brand activity contain any plausible visual clues that can be made into a meaningful symbol. In such cases, a designer must look to the key words in the brief for features that can be visually expressed. The words such as connection, speed, unity, network, care, stability, and balance can point you in a productive design direction.

Visual clues for logo design may also come from the naming rather than brand activity. For example, if the name of the brand is D4studios then the potential concept is hiding right in the naming. Letter *D* and number 4 have a strong visual appeal, so the monogram involving the two characters might be the best approach.

There are also times when the name of the brand in itself can make an interesting mark. For example, a brand named *Limoni* (a word that refers to lemon) may have a lemon as a symbol in the design. Some may argue that when a mark directly depicts the brand's name the approach is too straightforward, lacks cleverness, and is less attractive. Still, we must not forget that when a viewer sees a mark on its own, the name will be recalled automatically, and identification of the brand will be quicker.

Mood Boarding

Mood boards help a designer and a client get a sense of the stylistic directions a project can take. The goal is to get yourself excited about the project and get a glimpse of possibilities that can be developed.

A designer should not limit the mood board to the brand identity. Adding images of nature, architecture, painting, or other sources of inspiration can all provide good reference points and aid in the process of logo development. Let the project lead the mood boarding process to some extent.

As you create your mood board, compartmentalize styles in different sections of the board. For example, have images with a more classic direction grouped in one section, high-tech futuristic styles in another, colorful styles kept separate and monochromatic in a different group. This will create clear boundaries between directions. Similarly, place logo subcategories in separate groups—pictorial, letterform, monograms—accompanied with relevant imagery.

Mood boards can be shared with the client or made for your personal use. Some clients like to be engaged in the process more than others. My personal preference is to limit engagement because sometimes it can become a hindrance. Not all the clients have ability to foresee how the design will develop, and a mood direction they like initially may not be the one that turns out to create to the best final result.

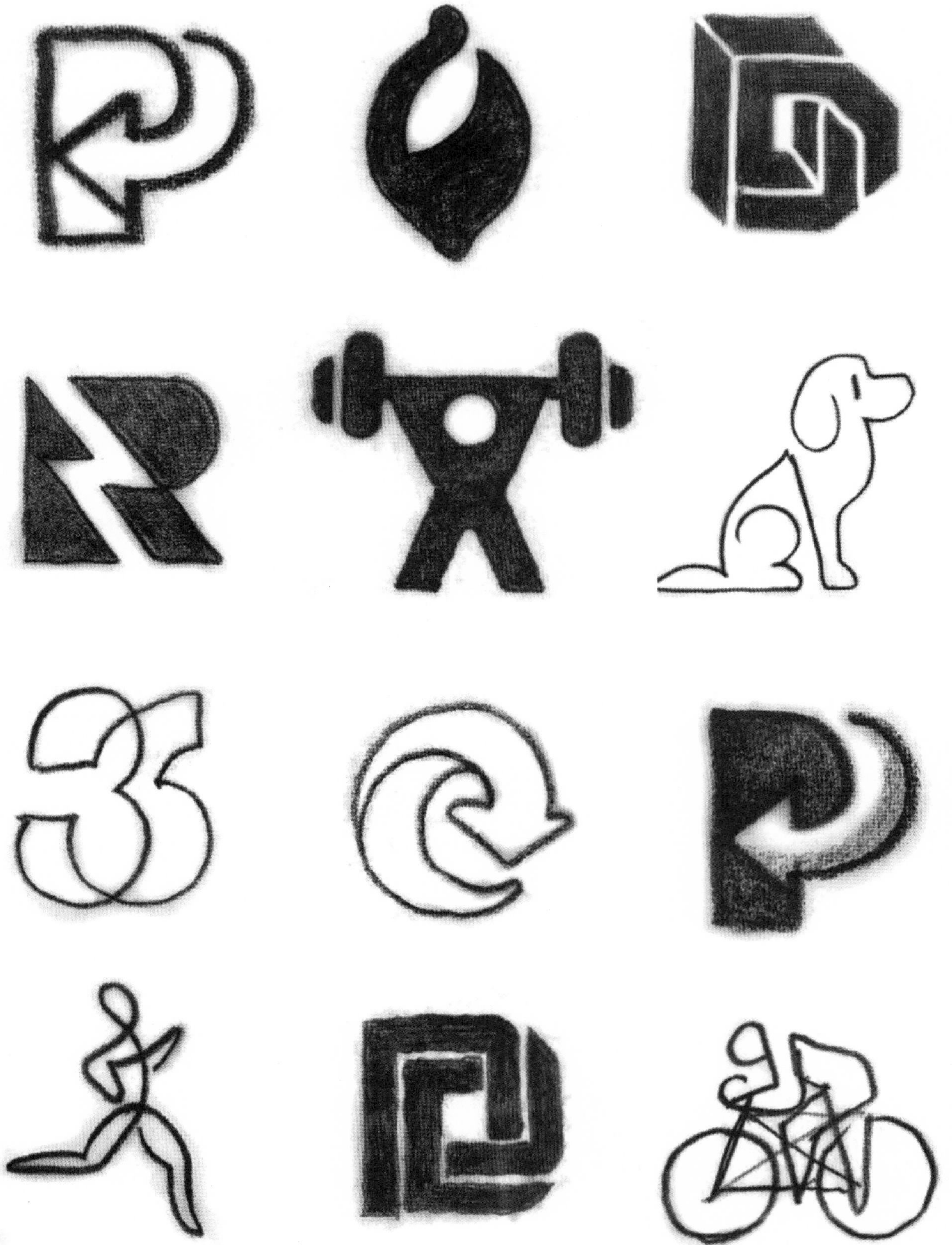

Sketching

Sketching is one of the essential parts of logo development. It allows a designer to express ideas freely. It also lets you get away from technology and engage in an activity that exercises your imagination, hand-eye coordination, and mindfulness.

Sketching is most useful as a way to create initial concepts without the hindrances of digital tools. For instance, when your imagination tries to generate an idea, your hand movement will attempt to reflect it, creating a corresponding form. Sketching makes this quick and natural.

To form the same initial ideas on a computer takes time. The logo design tools—the pen tool, in particular—do not have the same versatility and flexibility that pencil has. You'll need to create an outline using anchor points; move the anchors to the correct locations so the rough shape is visible; and adjust the anchors to achieve the desirable shape. It is complex and time consuming, making it hardly suitable for free creative output.

Divide the process into several stages. Start with sketching numerous rough concepts. Then study and refine the rough images. Finally, fine-tune the refined image, tracing it until the desired form is achieved and it's ready to be imported to a digital platform.

Examples of the fine-tuned sketches ready to be imported to a digital platform

The Initial Stage

For the initial stage, a designer must not fear making mistakes. Now is not the time to worry about the clarity, spacing, form, or silhouette. Instead sketching should be performed as a fever-like activity, pouring ideas on the paper. The more unrestrained, spontaneous, unconscious, and uninhibited, the better.

This should be viewed as an exploratory stage where anything is allowed. A designer must take time to experiment with various concepts, applying rough strokes, imperfect shapes, careless curves, and uncontrolled outlines. At the end of the process, the sketch paper should look like a battlefield of semiformed, unfinished chunks and pieces of concepts.

One may ask, what is the use of this? Isn't it better to take time and draw something more concise? The answer is yes and no. The initial stage is about quantity rather than quality. A concise sketch takes time and concentration. When we open up to spontaneous impulses, we can create any form we wish, allowing more free expression and, most importantly, allowing unexpected lucky accidents to occur.

(1) Examples of the initial sketching stage: Studies of uppercase letters *F* and *R*

(2) Examples of the initial sketching stage: Studies of uppercase letter *F*

1.

2.

The Refinement Stage

The refinement stage is one of the more exciting parts of the sketching process. Select the most appealing concept from the initial stage. It may be hard to judge how appropriate it is and how good it will be when finished. That's okay at this stage.

Begin by trusting a gut feeling. Go with the concept that feels like it has the most potential. At the start, the selected concept should be approximately 30 percent of what the final version will look like. The goal of this stage is to achieve an image that is 50 to 60 percent close to the final look. At this point a designer must be feeling they are on to something but that something needs to be owned, developed, and made familiar.

As a first step, redraw the chosen concept as an initial reference. After that, you'll make numerous similar sketches during this study phase; something new and improved must be tried with each new sketch. Here attention should be paid to how elements are interacting; balanced flow and outline must be achieved. This is also a chance for new combinations and accidents to happen.

Each new sketch should be compared to the previous one. This process allows a designer to get a sense of what parts are working and what parts are not. The undesired parts should be eliminated or substituted by desired parts.

Examples of how a sketch develops during the refinement process

The Fine-tuning Stage

Fine-tuning is the final and most precise part of the sketching process. Once the structure of the figure is achieved, using tracing paper, the form develops further. This allows a refinement of all the previous formal solutions and transforms the piece into something more complete.

At each step of this process, tracing paper must be used. Trace the initial image, then subsequent images should be traced again and again with minor improvements. These will be visible on every resulting traced image. The favorable solutions should be kept, and unfavorable must be discarded.

In the end the achieved form needs to be clean and precise. There should not be too many formal changes in the overall look and feel during the execution stage. After the fine-tuning is complete, take a photo or scan the sketch and import it to the digital platform for the execution. The imported images must be sharp and high in contrast.

Fine-tuned sketch ready to be imported
to a digital platform

1

2

3

4

Execution

All of the emails, phone calls, video conferences, and sketching up until this point have been important—but if your execution fails, they all fail. This stage requires patience as you create numerous versions of the logo, each only slightly different from the last. You should also get in the habit of using best practices every time you work: copy and paste, then manipulate.

The sketches you have made up to this point have likely been a few strokes of your pencil, just enough for you and the client to agree on the direction. Your sketch now needs to be converted into a digital file and fine-tuned even further. After scanning the sketch into a program such as Adobe Illustrator, trace the sketch with the pencil tool to create a digital sketch. Trial and error are an integral part of this process. You may find that you have spent several hours headed down a path that ends up being useless.

To save yourself frustration and time, follow these steps each time you make a change: Before you change anything on your digital sketch, copy and paste the image within the same file. After you make one change, copy and paste the image again. Paste each new iteration next to the previous one to show how the design has progressed. When you realize something is not working, you will be able to easily look back and see where things started going wrong.

1. Imported fine-tuned sketch 2. The initial digital outline 3. Defined proportions 4. Defined curves and formal elements

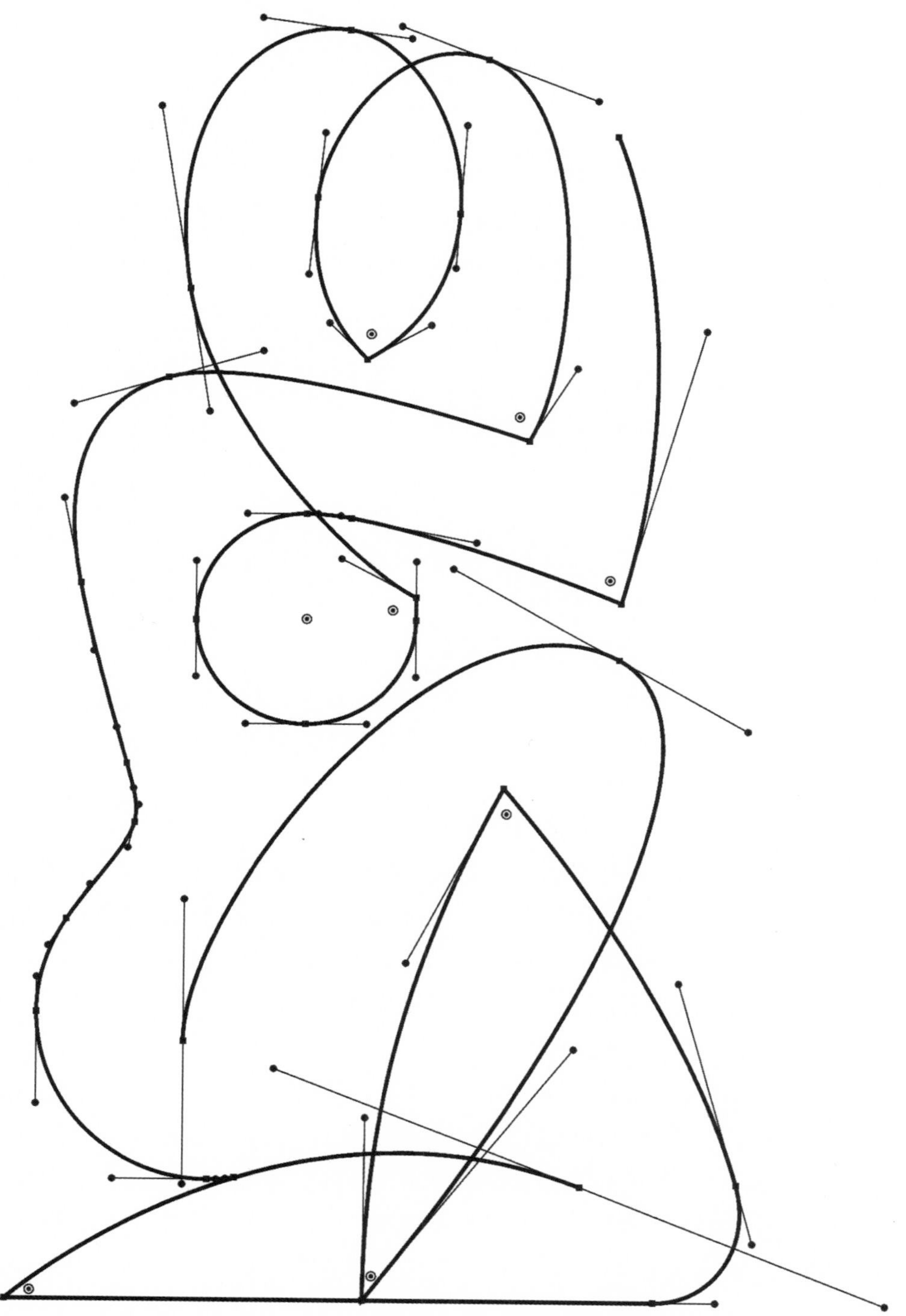

The final outcome with reduced anchor points, refined curves, and balanced proportions

The anchor points you created while digitizing your sketch will allow you to manipulate the image, to change the angle of a knee just so or smooth a rough line. Anchor points have great power and should be used sparingly—having too many can make your design look jagged. Stop periodically to check your anchor points and delete any that may be unnecessary.

Once you're happy with your design, you can begin the gridding process that is aimed at fixing, refining, and fine-tuning all the imperfections of the piece. As part of this process, use the shape tools to refine the shapes within your design: an ellipse to check that a curve is just right or a square to ensure the perfect corner. Aim for whole numbers for the degree of each angle; it's hard to explain why, but there's something mildly jarring about an odd angle. For the same reason, aim for whole numbers when finalizing the CMYK balance of your colors.

As a key part of any company's branding, logos are hugely important—they are also relatively small and simple, leaving little room for any error on the part of the designer. Before sending final files to your client, run through a final checklist:

1. Recheck anchors and remove any duplicate or unnecessary points.

2. Ensure all angles—particularly those around the outside border—are accurate.

3. Save all of your working files in your personal archives.

4. Refer to your original contract to ensure you've saved your deliverables as the appropriate sizes and file types.

5. Create an invoice for any remaining balance the client owes you.

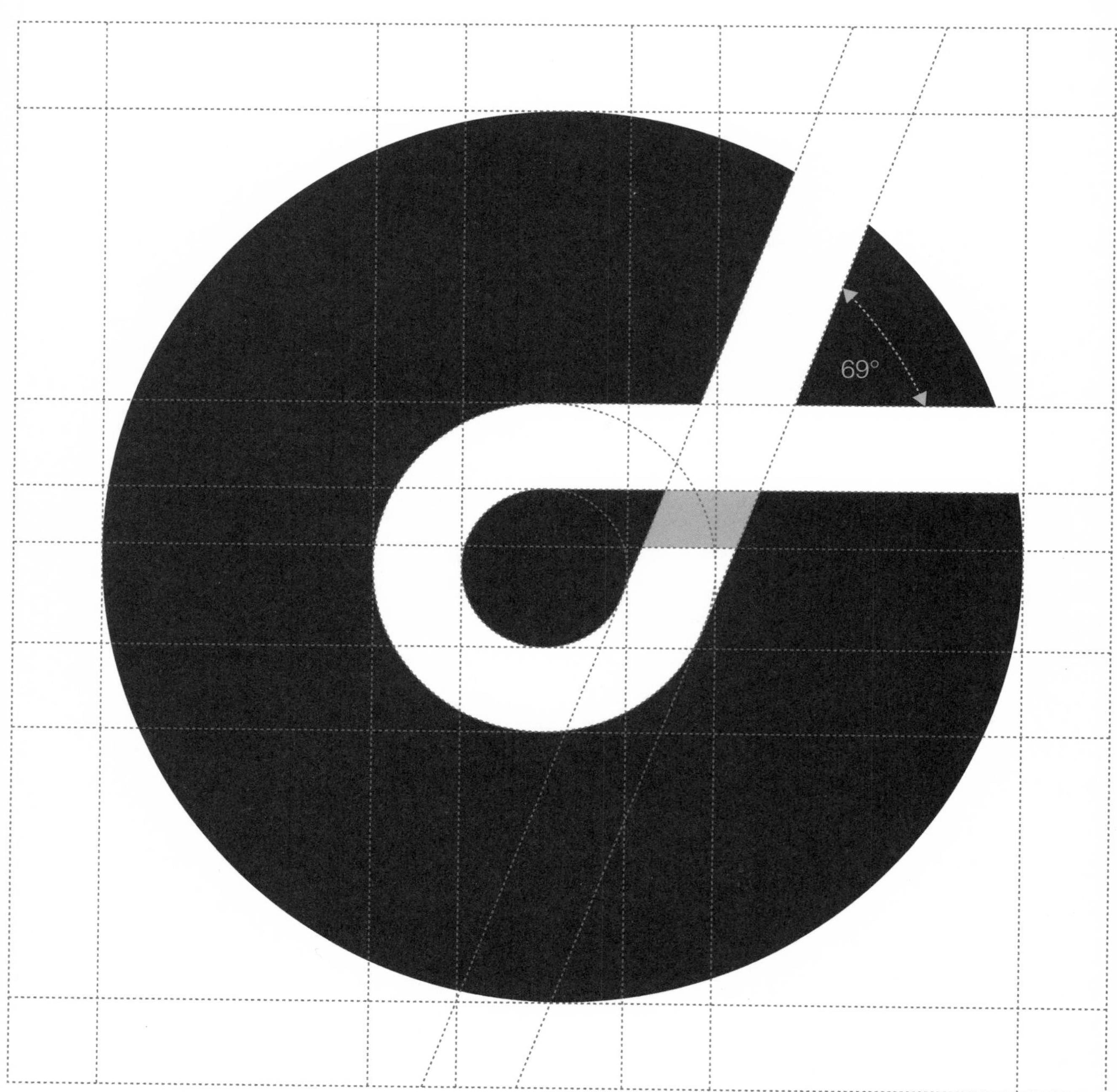
69°

Gridding

Gridding is the final part of a logo design process. It is aimed at fixing, refining, and fine-tuning all the imperfections of the piece. The process consists of applying geometric grids to the work so inconsistencies are noticed and fixed. The time to do gridding is after the work is finished and approved by a client. The adjustments to the logo after the gridding usually are too minimal to be noticed by a viewer.

Regardless of how precise a designer tries to be during the process, at a prefinal stage of logo development, there may be inconsistencies in the piece. Some elements might not be aligned; basic shapes might not be perfect or proportional; some angles and spacings might be off balance.

The first step is ensuring the elements are aligned. Examine the work to see if all parts of the design flow. The horizontal and vertical lines must be checked to see if there is any fluctuation in degrees: often the lines are 1 or 2 degrees off due to small technical mistakes on a designer's part. If the angle of an element is 43 degrees, care must be taken to make it 45. Changes in a few degrees rarely affect the work drastically; a 45-degree angle is more familiar to our cognitive faculties, therefore, more preferable.

The same approach applies to lines that are 90 or 0 degrees. If a certain angle is, for example, 33.46 degrees, then it is preferable to round it up to 35. This precision demonstrates that designed elements in the piece are carefully placed and not randomly made.

Construction grid for the Alpahmaetry logo. Fintech industry (France)

Next page: Seagull mark for the soccer club

Gridding Complex Forms

If something does not work within the grid, make it work outside the grid. Some marks with organic forms contain complex curves that cannot be gridded with simple geometric shapes. In such cases, it is unnecessary to grid those elements.

Gridding is a tool that helps the designer to adjust and align elements, but some parts of the logo may be too complex and do not need to be aligned with other elements. It's okay to leave these alone. Too many grids make a work look confusing, especially if they are unnecessary.

In complex organic figures, some curves appear unsuited for gridding simply because they don't consist of circles or ovals but are instead the combinations of several round shapes.

After the alignment and angles are fixed, the simple geometric shapes need to be grided: circles, squares, triangles, rectangles, ellipses. Make certain that a circle is a perfect circle, and a square is a perfect square. Now is the time for all the small inconsistencies and technical mistakes to be adjusted. The elements should be centered and aligned in accordance with the composing shapes.

Crane logo with construction grids

Next page: Whale logo with overused construction grids

Next page after: *W* letterform and its construction grid

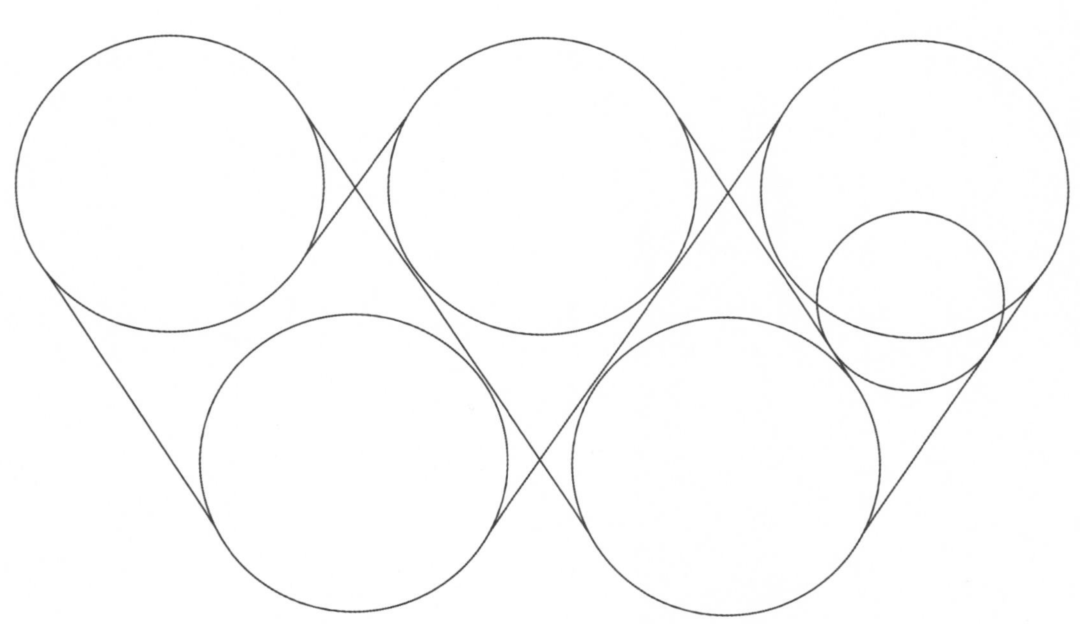

MINIO

Type Lockup

The type lockup stage involves finalizing the positioning and relative sizes of all logo elements (e.g., icon, wordmark, tagline, etc.). Once these elements are locked up, they should not be taken apart or altered.

Multiple lockups should be created for each brand, giving the client the flexibility to easily adapt to various media, sizes, and uses. A lockup for use on a letterhead may consist of multiple elements, while one for a mobile website may be just the icon. The complexity of each element should be considered as the size of the lockup shrinks—an intricate logo may not be legible at small sizes and should be simplified.

Balance is essential for a well-designed lockup. An ornate logo should be accompanied by a plain, sans serif font. Bold elements should be countered by thin elements. This balance creates a visual contrast between elements and allows you to view each one independently. The aim, however, is not contrast for the sake of contrast—each element should complement the others. If a certain peculiar element of the symbol, such as curvature, can be applied to the type, then care must be taken that it's done in a manner that subtly reflects the symbol.

Finalizing a lockup can feel like a tedious task filled with small changes of questionable importance. The difference between bold and slightly-more-bold text or a slight tweak to kerning may not be readily apparent to most people, but they are the difference between a good designer and a great designer. As you become more experienced, these details will become second nature and will require less of your time.

Min.io cloud services (type lockup)

Next page: ACT; research center

Next page after: Georgian Railway (type lockup)

Lockup of the Symbol and the Type

The corporate signature consists of the sybol and the logotype in a balanced relationship. Neue Haas Unica was selected as a typeface for the English version of the logotype. The Georgian version of the typeface was created in accordance with the principles of Neue Haas Unica.

The cap height of the type is same size as the thickness of the horizontal blocks of the monogram. No changes are allowed in the spaing, the letter form, or the proportions of the logotype

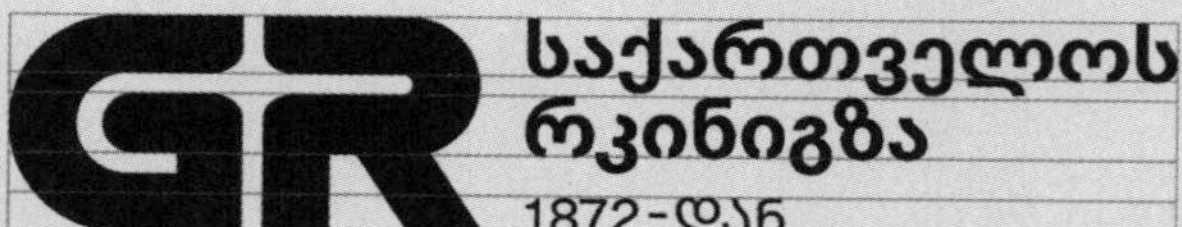

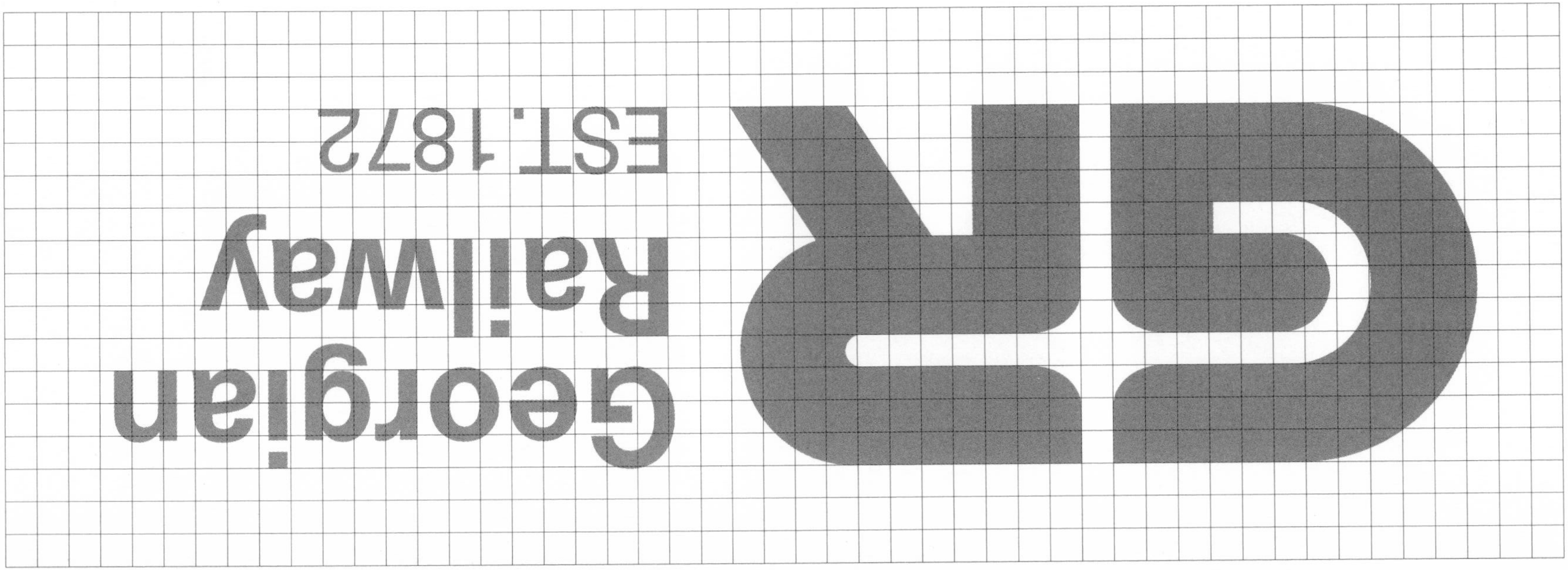

Georgian
Railway
EST.1872

Chapter 5
Presentation

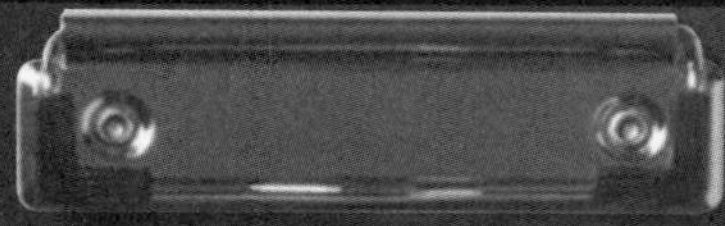

Kourtney Parra
(407) 878-5542
226 Washington Ave
Lake Mary, Florida(FL)
kourtney
@aiera.com
Date:
03.07.2019
To:
Scott Rivera
scott.r@hello.com
Lorem ipsum dolor sit amet, consectetur adipiscing elit. Nullam euismod ac dui a vestibulum. Aenean eleifend malesuada est nec dictum. Nullam ac vehicula dui, et maximus nisi. Nulla rutrum lorem mattis interdum rutrum. Nam dolor turpis, blandit ac nunc scelerisque, pulvinar dignissim est.
Nunc ut augue ac sapien ultrices consequat. Suspendisse mollis faucibus neque. Nullam cursus lectus et justo fringilla, quis sodales mi semper. Sed facilisis purus eget tellus suscipit tempus. Donec eu mauris commodo, tempor risus vitae, ullamcorper leo. Praesent tincidunt scelerisque laoreet. Duis cursus lacus dolor, vitae lacinia metus pellentesque vitae. Ut molestie libero ipsum, at convallis sapien pulvinar et. Mauris dignissim nisi vitae lacus venenatis.
Integer neque nisl, congue quis leo eget, accumsan accumsan ipsum. Nunc gravida facilisis massa non fringilla. In iaculis nulla a velit gravida iaculis. In nulla dolor, sodales a maximus quis, euismod tristique dui. Donec ultrices metus non felis condimentum iaculis. Morbi egestas porta dui, sit amet consequat libero malesuada nec. Aenean id ex in nunc interdum porta et et purus. Proin ac elit varius, scelerisque risus eget, tempor lectus. Etiam placerat facilisis arcu, at lobortis dolor. Quisque condimentum pretium libero vitae lobortis. Proin posuere porttitor nibh, vel hendrerit felis porttitor nec.
Morbi eleifend auctor varius. Quisque nisi eros, commodo nec mollis at, tempus at eros. Proin mollis dolor et quam rutrum.
Kourtney

Kourtney Parra
Building Architect
Partner
226 Washington Ave
Lake Mary, Florida(FL)
(407)
878-5542
kourtney
@aiera.com

Kourtney Parra
Building Architect
Partner
226 Washington Ave
Lake Mary, Florida(FL)
(407)
878-5542
kourtney
@aiera.com

Presentation

You usually need to make three presentations for a project. The first should include three initial designs, and each should be semi-complete. I like to present them at about 80 percent finalized, in grayscale. This initial showing of work is a place to discuss any concerns, ideas, or general thoughts.

At this stage, it is important to bring the client's focus away from communicating deep ideas about their brand. Deep ideas require more storytelling than a logo can provide. Instead the goal should be to communicate something about the brand as quickly and simply as possible.

Identity elements for Aiera (artificial intelligence industry), June 2020

Next page: Identity element for the Mega-Bridge (cryptocurrency exchange platform), April 2021

Meera Von Caghan
Law Advisor/CEO
Partner
+61
03 7010 5678
889 BU st Melbourne,
VIC, Australia 9000
meera
@megabridge.com
Date:
01.08.2021
To:
Zakariya Thomas
zakariya@hello.com

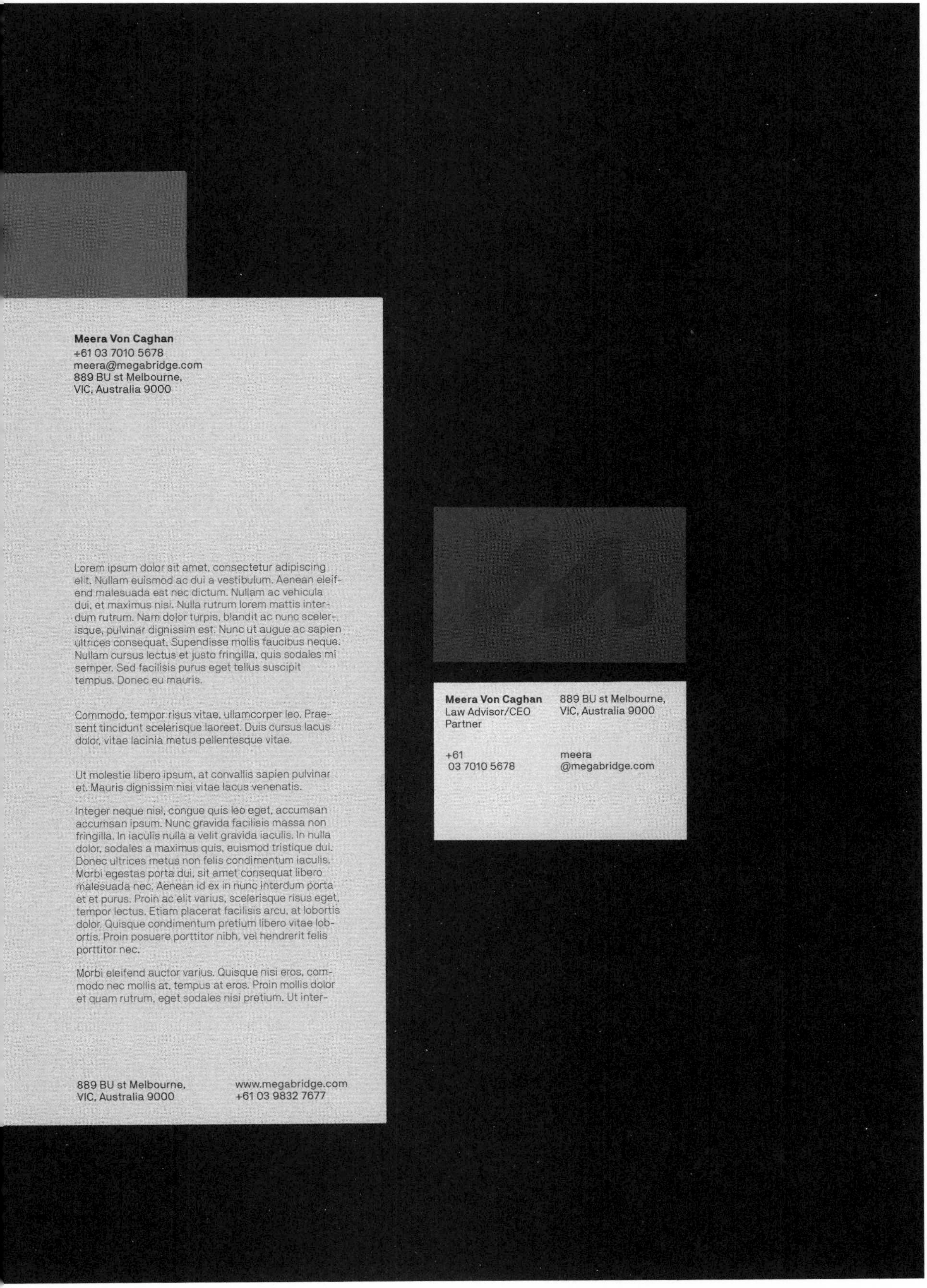

Meera Von Caghan
+61 03 7010 5678
meera@megabridge.com
889 BU st Melbourne,
VIC, Australia 9000

Lorem ipsum dolor sit amet, consectetur adipiscing elit. Nullam euismod ac dui a vestibulum. Aenean eleifend malesuada est nec dictum. Nullam ac vehicula dui, et maximus nisi. Nulla rutrum lorem mattis interdum rutrum. Nam dolor turpis, blandit ac nunc scelerisque, pulvinar dignissim est. Nunc ut augue ac sapien ultrices consequat. Supendisse mollis faucibus neque. Nullam cursus lectus et justo fringilla, quis sodales mi semper. Sed facilisis purus eget tellus suscipit tempus. Donec eu mauris.

Commodo, tempor risus vitae, ullamcorper leo. Praesent tincidunt scelerisque laoreet. Duis cursus lacus dolor, vitae lacinia metus pellentesque vitae.

Ut molestie libero ipsum, at convallis sapien pulvinar et. Mauris dignissim nisi vitae lacus venenatis.

Integer neque nisl, congue quis leo eget, accumsan accumsan ipsum. Nunc gravida facilisis massa non fringilla. In iaculis nulla a velit gravida iaculis. In nulla dolor, sodales a maximus quis, euismod tristique dui. Donec ultrices metus non felis condimentum iaculis. Morbi egestas porta dui, sit amet consequat libero malesuada nec. Aenean id ex in nunc interdum porta et et purus. Proin ac elit varius, scelerisque risus eget, tempor lectus. Etiam placerat facilisis arcu, at lobortis dolor. Quisque condimentum pretium libero vitae lobortis. Proin posuere porttitor nibh, vel hendrerit felis porttitor nec.

Morbi eleifend auctor varius. Quisque nisi eros, commodo nec mollis at, tempus at eros. Proin mollis dolor et quam rutrum, eget sodales nisi pretium. Ut inter-

889 BU st Melbourne,
VIC, Australia 9000

www.megabridge.com
+61 03 9832 7677

Meera Von Caghan
Law Advisor/CEO
Partner

889 BU st Melbourne,
VIC, Australia 9000

+61
03 7010 5678

meera
@megabridge.com

The way you choose to present work to clients is ultimately up to your preference. There is, however, some consistency in presentations that is expected within the industry. Your first slide should include the name of the company you are designing for, the names of all of the designers who worked on the project, the name of the project and the date. Your second slide should include some basic background about your studio and overview of the insights about the project.

With the third slide, I start sharing designs. At this stage in the presentation process, I show only grayscale designs. I will present a full-scale design with a description of the concepts, followed by five to six mock-ups for each of the three designs I am presenting so the client can get used to the form. Your mock-ups should be practical and based on the company—use cups for a mock-up for a coffeehouse, not for a gym. It's also preferable to have all the mock-ups similar in style.

After your client has settled on one of your designs and provided their initial feedback, the next stage is coloring. With colors, I usually research what the competitor brands are using and try *not* to match their palate. Sometimes clients have strong preferences in which case I simply comply. With simple marks, it's easier to deal with colors because usually there are fewer colors and color combinations to manage.

After the final selection has been made, the working files of logos on various backgrounds (color and monochrome) need to be prepared. The final files should be in .ai, .pdf, .eps, and high-resolution .jpg and .png formats. Those five options are enough for any project.

Hoodie for the MegaBridge (cryptocurrency exchange platform)

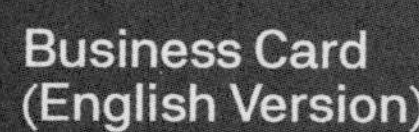

Business Card (English Version)

Business card layout shall be constructed in accordance to given template. Print file will be attached to the ACT Brand Guidelines for further use.

Name/Surname	Helvetica LT std (Black).
Position/Info	Helvetica LT std (Black).
Contacts	Helvetica LT std (Bold).

SKY WALKER

Executive Producer

Brand Guidelines

Most clients—a lot of start-ups with limited resources, for example—don't ask for brand guidelines. And they may not see their inherent value during the initial stages of their company's development. For a sizable company that expects to see its branding appearing across a large variety of mediums, a set of brand guidelines, or a brand book, is an absolute necessity. Most of the big brands make the wise investment in brand guidelines. The guidelines can consist of several sections, but we will focus on six.

Brand guidelines can help clients distinguish between the print and digital roles of its branding. Even for brands with minimal needs, the smallest package will give the client the logo on various backgrounds in both print and digital formats. But oftentimes they will not know which logo to use when and will unknowingly send their digital logo to their stationery printer, for instance.

Business card for FEVR (motion graphic studio)

Kerning

The rectangle grid was used as the basis of the construction of the symbol. the space between letters 'e' and 't' was chosen as an x unit. Spacing between other letters were composed in accordance to the chosen x unit.

europebet

3x 2.5x 3x x 2.5x 2x 2.5x 2x x

1. Logo Use Guidelines

This section is the most important, and I advise every brand to have guidelines for using its logo. The guidelines should define when and how to use the logo on the most common backgrounds: black logo on white backgrounds, white logo on black backgrounds, and using the logo on colored and pattered/photo backgrounds. This section should also explain the most common pitfalls associated with logo design and usage.

Kerning

If the logo includes type, then the guidelines must address kerning, or the spacing between letters, within the context of several settings. If you typed a brand such as Coca-Cola in Helvetica, for example, the kerning is well balanced from the start and would look fine typed out. But not all fonts are as well balanced from the start, and just because the spacing between letters in the logo may work well in headings in a book, for instance, that does not mean that same spacing can be applied elsewhere. Therefore the designer must always be on the lookout for instances when the spacing can be fixed or tightened up and improved so everything looks evenly spaced.

Although this technology has improved over the past forty years and it's easier to adjust, these important spacing details need to be a part of the guidelines because you never know when they

Type kerning for Europebet (online gambling site)

Logotype: Incorrect Uses

The logotype is designed to be shown free-standing horizontally against a solid neutral background. The logotype must not be altered or distorted in any way. The effectiveness of the logotype depends on consistently correct usage as outlined in this manual.

The examples shown below illustrate some incorrect uses of the logotype:

1. The logotype should never be shown outlined.
2. The logotype must never be placed within another outline shape, such as a box.
3. Do not change the logotype colors.
4. Do not use the blend tool.
5. Do not change an angle of the logotype.
6. No patterns should be used within the logotype.

1

2

3

4

5

6

might be needed. For example, Europebet had signage on top of a building that was approximately 65 feet (20 meters) long, so they needed some measurement conversions that could be applied to the logo at that size. Fortunately they had those measurements in their logo use guidelines.

Dos and Don'ts

I usually include a Dos and Don'ts section because frequently in-house designers like to take liberties—rotating/tilting things or adding effects—so I want to instruct them to not alter the logo in any way. And the advice in this section provides the company's designers with guardrails for using the logo creatively but without alterations.

Minimum Sizes

Sometimes when a logo is run too small it loses its visibility or clarity. In the studio, we experiment with the logo first and reduce it to determine at what point it starts to lose its identifiable elements. Once the designer determines the point where the logo has lost its clarity, the measurement just before that is added to the guidelines as the minimum size. For instance, if the logo loses its clarity at 3 mm, the guidelines will state that the logo cannot run at a size less than that on either their digital or print materials.

Exclusion Zone

The exclusion zone is the area where the logo needs to be free of any other graphic elements. If the logo is to be clear and effective it needs to have established boundaries. If something intrudes in that area, whether that be another logo or illustration, the results will not be pleasing. This zone should be based on an element in

Dos and don'ts; ACT research company

Next page: Minimum size and exclusion zone for Georgia Made by Characters (Guest of Honour, Frankfurt Book Fair)

Minimum size

For legibility reasons, a minimum size at which the logo may be reproduced is recommended, the logo should never be any smaller than 4 millimeters.

23mm

Georgia
Made by Characters
Guest of Honour
Frankfurter Buchmesse 2018

17mm

Georgia
Made by Characters
Guest of Honour
Frankfurter Buchmesse 2018

12mm

Georgia
Made by Characters
Guest of Honour
Frankfurter Buchmesse 2018

8mm

Georgia
Made by Characters
Guest of Honour
Frankfurter Buchmesse 2018

4mm

Exclusion Zone

The 'exclusion zone' refers to the area around the logo which must remain free from other copy to ensure that the logo is not obscured. The signature must be always surrounded by a minimum amount of "breathing space". No text, graphic, photographic, illustrative or typographic element must encroach upon this space. have a margin of clear space on all sides around it equal to the x height of the chosen typography. No other elements (text, images, other logos, puppy GIFs, etc.) can appear inside this clear space.

Secondary Colors

Secondary brand colors were selected in relation to the primary Europebet orange so that vibrantcy and distinctness is maintained throughout various mediums.

R:60 G:205 B:0

R:250 G:170 B:65

R:240 G:90 B:40

R:230 G:105 B:170

R:235 G:0 B:140

R:150 G:40 B:140

R:140 G:100 B:170

R:10 G:120 B:190

R:0 G:165 B:225

R:75 G:190 B:150

R:170 G:219 B:110

R:230 G:230 B:40

the logo. Here, we used the radius of the circle to create an exclusion zone. (If we used a fixed measurement, such as 4 inches [10 cm] for instance, that distance would no longer apply to a logo that is running very large.)

Background Colors

If the client's logo is pink or orange, it would never be advisable to run that logo on a blue background because that's not a complementary color and it is going to negatively affect the visibility. The logo use guidelines should also include a device that clearly establishes the backgrounds that offer optimal visibility and exclusion zones.

2. Primary Colors and Secondary Colors

Every brand uses at least one primary color, and often clients will also need appropriate secondary colors. Whether you're providing primary colors, secondary colors, or both, give the client with CMYK codes, RGB codes, hex codes, and Pantone numbers.

Some brands *only* have a primary color. Chase Bank, for example, has its blue and that blue is everywhere. But there are cases where they need secondary colors—for interiors of printed materials, for example. Secondary colors usually complement the primary color, and brands will use stronger more saturated colors (for as little as 5 or 10 percent of the design). These creates some differentiation in printed materials or can be used as highlights elsewhere.

Provide four or five complementary colors for brands to use as secondary color options. For this example although the client did not request a lot of secondary colors, I provided several neon secondary colors for use throughout its online gambling platform. I included more

Europebet (online gambling site) secondary color palate

Typography

Neue Haas Unica Pro

45pt regular

1234
5678
90

colors than are typically provided in brand guidelines, but in this case the project called for a spectrum of colors.

If you don't have access to the Pantone catalog, Adobe Illustrator has a simple tool to convert the CMYK colors into Pantone colors for you. If your client has the resources, they should invest in Pantone colors; this is what I advise my clients. The Pantone colors are better and cleaner; they don't fade, and they don't transfer to another paper if they are not dry. They should be the go-to colors for your clients who can afford them.

3. Typography

When it comes to logo type, corporate typography is often a different entity—though not always. Most of the time I advise clients use a simple sans serif because it's neutral, simple to use, and most devices have it has a default font, meaning it will not be an additional cost. Corporate type must be simple and readable; it must also use a neutral sans serif type for main text. Clients also need header or title type for use on posters, brochures, and covers of other printed materials. This is where the designer is allowed more freedom and can use whatever they believe will provide the proper contrast to the main text or body type.

4. Grids

InDesign is the best tool for creating your grids and they should be based on either the A4 format or letter-size format (United States). The squarer your grid boxes are, the more versatile your grids will be. Grids that feature more rectangular shaped boxes, for instance, limit the options for placing various graphical elements or text—limits that don't exist when your grid boxes are square. Also make sure your margins and gutters are done thoughtfully, as opposed to relying on InDesign's default settings.

Typography; Numbers. Georgia Made by Characters (Guest of Honour, Frankfurt Book Fair)

Next page: Logo use guidelines; Graphic device; Georgian railways

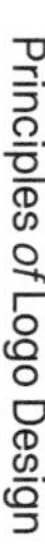

Logotype on Different Backgrounds

The Georgian Railway corporate color is red (Pantone 48-8 U). Whenever the application (Pantone 48-8 U). Whenever the application logo should appear red on white, or white on red. If red is not available, the logo may be black on white, or white on black. Contrast must always be sufficient.

When reproducing the logotype for print on photographic background, care must be taken to ensure that the area surrounding the logotype is tonally even and either sufficiently light or sufficiently dark to ensure the logotype is legible.

GR Georgian Railway EST. 1872

GR Georgian Railway EST. 1872

GR Georgian Railway EST. 1872

Logotype 1.9

Business Card (English Version)

Business card layout shall be constructed in accordance to given template. Print file will be attached to the ACT Brand Guidelines for further use.

Name/Surname	15pt, FF Mark (Heavy).
Position/Info	9pt, FF Mark (Regular).
Contacts	9pt, FF Mark (Bold).

Ketevan Gaprindashvili
Regional Coordinator
Imereti-racha/lechkhumi-kvemo svaneti

Mobile: (+995 577) 77 69 77
E-Mail: k.gaprindashvili@act-global.com

Address: 8 Jon (Malkhaz)
Shalikashvili str.
Web: www.act-global.com

Ketevan Gaprindashvili
Regional Coordinator
Imereti-racha/lechkhumi-kvemo svaneti

Mobile: (+995 577) 77 69 77
E-Mail: k.gaprindashvili@act-global.com

Address: 8 Jon (Malkhaz)
Shalikashvili str.
Web: www.act-global.com

5. Graphic Devices

We discuss graphic devices in much more detail in chapter 3, but in the context of the brand guidelines it is important to explain that the ratios of the graphic device and the logo should be similar. In other words, if the logo is a square format, then the graphic device should be a ratio of that square shape; or if it's more rectangular shaped then the graphic device should be more rectangular. (A square logo in a rectangular device or rectangular logo in a square device will create distracting amount of space around the logo.)

6. Stationery

The three most popular stationery design requests made by most brands these days are for business cards, letterhead, and folders. Envelopes used to be requested very often, but fewer and fewer companies are mailing materials and so requests for envelopes have dropped sharply in recent years.

Business Cards

Business cards must use the corporate type because the goal is to use this type on all of their materials. The face of the business card should be clean and free of a lot of graphic elements, and it should only state what the client has requested. The less information on the business card the better and the quicker it communicates. It's a small space, and if there's too much information it can become hard to read and a little overwhelming.

Ideally the front of the business card should list a name, title, phone number (if they want), and email address. Sometimes clients want the company's physical address on the front, but that kind of information is easily accessible on the corporate website so encourage them to

Stationery; Business card design; ACT research company

Invoice

Invoice layout shall be constructed in accordance to given template. Print file will be attached to the ACT Brand Guidelines for further use.

include a URL on the back of the card instead. Also, if the brand identity includes patterns of any kind, then those should appear on the back of the card. If there are no patterns, stick with the primary color.

If business cards are printed cheaply, the results are never good. Advise your clients to use thicker paper, lamination or finishing (to reduce wear and tear), and maybe some embossing. This relatively small piece of stationery can make a disproportionately large impression on those who encounter it.

Letterhead

Although some companies insist on printing the letterhead on their laser printers, not all companies have that option, so encourage your client to use a printing house whenever possible to achieve optimal results. The header of the letterhead offers more space than a business card, so this is an opportunity for the client to display more information. There should not be anything printed on the back of the letterhead, because the colors and will run through to the front unless the paper stock is very thick. Instead keep it simple and keep it clean.

Folders

The designer needs to take the lead on this phase of the project: you should direct the graphic design on folders *and* the physical design of the folders. Several online resources perform this function, but the knife that cuts out this design should be that of the designer. (In reality this is often done with lasers, but the point remains the same.)

Some designers may go their whole careers without seeing a brand book, but for those brands that have committed significant resources and the designers behind them, the results are invaluable.

Stationery; invoice design; ACT research company

Next page: Stationery; Ticket design; Georgian Railways

International Tickets

International Tickets

გისურვებთ სასიამოვნო მგზავრობას

Have a nice trip

Please note that departures are indicated in local time. Please check the date and time of departure.

Passengers when boarding the train should present a valid ticket to the conductor and a document proving their identity, or documents confirming the right to discounts if the passenger is entitled to such privileges.

Every passenger is entitled to bring aboard luggage not exceeding 36 kg in weight. The sum of the hand luggage's three dimensions must not exceed 180 cm;

Lost, damaged, or stolen tickets are non-refundable and cannot be exchanged.

Unused ticket may be returned only by the person registered in the ticket, based on the identity insurance card;

Unused tickets should be returned to a ticket office the train passes, in accordance with the relevant national rules of the railway service.

Желаем приятной поездки

На проездном документе указано время отправления поезда, действующее на железной дороге государства отправления.
Проверьте дату и время отправления поезда.

При посадке в поезд необходимо иметь проездной документ и документ удостоверяющий личность, а при наличии льгот – документ подтверждающий право на льготный проезд;

Пассажир имеет право перевозить с собой на один проездной документ ручную кладь весом не более 36 кг, размер которой в сумме трех измерений не превышает 180 см;

Утерянные, испорченные пассажиром проездные документы не восстанавливаются и уплаченная за них сумма не возвращается;

Неиспользованный проездной документ принимается к возврату только от пассажира на имя которого оформлен документ, при предъявлении документа удостоверяющего личность пассажира;

Возврат неиспользованных проездных документов производится в билетных кассах пути следования поезда, согласно правилам соответствующей железной дороги.

#58-3838

გისურვებთ სასიამოვნო მგზავრობას

Have a nice trip

Please note that departures are indicated in local time. Please check the date and time of departure.

Passengers when boarding the train should present a valid ticket to the conductor and a document proving their identity, or documents confirming the right to discounts if the passenger is entitled to such privileges.

Every passenger is entitled to bring aboard luggage not exceeding 36 kg in weight. The sum of the hand luggage's three dimensions must not exceed 180 cm;

Lost, damaged, or stolen tickets are non-refundable and cannot be exchanged.

Unused ticket may be returned only by the person registered in the ticket, based on the identity insurance card;

Unused tickets should be returned to a ticket office the train passes, in accordance with the relevant national rules of the railway service.

Желаем приятной поездки

На проездном документе указано время отправления поезда, действующее на железной дороге государства отправления.
Проверьте дату и время отправления поезда.

При посадке в поезд необходимо иметь проездной документ и документ удостоверяющий личность, а при наличии льгот – документ подтверждающий право на льготный проезд;

Пассажир имеет право перевозить с собой на один проездной документ ручную кладь весом не более 36 кг, размер которой в сумме трех измерений не превышает 180 см;

Утерянные, испорченные пассажиром проездные документы не восстанавливаются и уплаченная за них сумма не возвращается;

Неиспользованный проездной документ принимается к возврату только от пассажира на имя которого оформлен документ, при предъявлении документа удостоверяющего личность пассажира;

Возврат неиспользованных проездных документов производится в билетных кассах пути следования поезда, согласно правилам соответствующей железной дороги.

#58-3838

The structure of your offering will also inform your pricing. How many designs are you presenting to a client? What is the time frame for the project? How many iterations are needed?

I recommend presenting three initial concepts to a client at a time. Even if you have developed five or ten during your design process, it is best to present a few better ones to avoid overwhelming the client. Three well-developed concepts are better than a dozen half-developed ones. And providing too many designs can come off as a lack of confidence on your part.

Designers should start out knowing their base rate and how long it takes to develop one concept. For a beginner, I advise having a base rate in rough accordance with the time it takes to develop one concept. Your base rate and hourly rate together will inform how much you will charge a client. Your time is valuable, and your pricing should reflect that.

For the experienced designer, I advise having a flat rate per project. After decades of experience, sometimes high-quality concepts appear quickly; it does not make sense to have an hourly rate for the years of accumulated knowledge.

In some cases, a client may give you a budget. If you're a beginner, you can use their parameters to better inform your pricing. You may also use the parameters to inform what you will be able to provide as a design package. What you charge may fluctuate based on your client. For example, a start-up or small business will likely see a smaller charge than a mid-level business and the mid-level will be charged less than a well-established corporation.

I sometimes take on passion projects—projects where I receive less than my regular rate. These are important to me for the work the company does or the unique challenge the project presents. I recommend having a minimum fee for these situations. But, if a client cannot meet your lowest fee, there are other scenarios where a more equal exchange can be made. For example, you may ask a start-up whom you find promising and believe in for equity in the company. Yes, a logo designer rarely gets a large share, but engaging with a few companies here and there can add up to a sizable passive income.

The most important thing to remember for pricing is that your rates should never be stagnant. The more projects you complete, the better understanding you will have of the work each project requires and clients' expectations when it comes to rates. If clients eagerly agree to your rates, you might not be charging enough.

After each completed project, try to increase your rate to test the limits of the value of your work. For example, if you are working on several projects at one time and a new client approaches, give them significantly higher than your usual price. If the client disagrees then you have little to lose because financially you are already set with your other projects. If the client agrees, then you must do extra work, and at the same time you get a better idea of the market value of your work. If the workload is too high, you can always ask your trusted fellow designers to help with parts of the project, perhaps concepting or sketching. In the end, execution, fine-tuning, and art direction must be yours in order to stay on fair ground with the client.

Here and there, you may agree to do a project for free for a loved one or a nonprofit organization, especially if you are a beginner and it's a fun project for interesting people. After all, it's pleasurable to design identities and the more exposure your work gets, the better it is for future success.

F 10XR
F 10XR
US

Design Studio

Designers—if we truly see ourselves as creatives—need to establish a creative a space where we feel comfortable. This is essential to achieving the type of concentration for long periods of time that you need to perform your best work.

Your goal should be a space that your brain reflexively recognizes as your comfort zone; it is the place where you always go to create things. I advise any designer just starting out to do what I did with the first money I earned: invest in a studio space. It is the best investment for your psychological health and your future productivity.

The design studio cannot be full of meaningless objects; designers need to live in the design space. This means design objects—and only design objects—should make up that space. Bring in your favorite chair, your favorite table, your favorite books, and whatever else you need to immerse yourself in an environment in which from every point in the studio you live as a designer.

This need not be an expensive endeavor. Nowadays it is much more affordable to surround yourself with good design objects. As long as it feels different for you when you are in the studio compared to anywhere else, and it was created by you for you, the results will be revealed in your creative output.

Studio George Bokhua

Next page: A library; Studio George Bokhua

Sagmeister: Another Book...
THE ELEMENTS OF TYPOGRAPHIC STYLE
ROBERT BRINGHURST
logolounge MASTERlibrary
マーク・シンボル 4
マーク・シンボル 3
PAUL KLEE
The Book of American Trade Marks
Karl Gerstner
THE ELEMENTS OF COLOR
TRADEMARK AND MONOGRAM SUGGESTIONS
ALBERTO GIACOMETTI
THE MUSEUM OF MODERN ART, NEW YORK
PICTOGRAM DESIGN
MODERN MONOGRAMS
Armin Hofmann
Zeichensysteme
Aicher Krampen
Swiss Made
Painting Abstraction: New Elements in Abstract Painting by Bob Nickas
HUMAN DIMENSION & INTERIOR SPACE
GEOMETRIC GRAPHICS
Хуан Миро. Образы
LOGOTYPES OF THE WORLD
YASABURO KUWAYAMA
KASHIWA SHOBO
KLEE & KANDINSKY
PRESTEL
IDENTITY: CHERMAYEFF & GEISMAR & HAVIV
TYPE
A-Z
SANS SERIF
A-Z
3000 ANIMAL & MYTHOLOGY LOGOS
logolounge MASTERlibrary
Designing Corporate Symbols
Carter
Stiebner Urban
Signs+Emblems
AKIRA 3
TD 63-73
diagrams
graphs
Michael Bierut How to
BANKING SYMBOLS
INTERECHO PRESS
BANKING SYMBOLS
INTERECHO PRESS
Signet Signal Symbol
Walter Diethelm
Pictogram and Icon Collection
Corporate Identity
Spring-Summer
SSENSE
Cards Against Humanity
CRANIUM

Top symbols and trademarks of the world
Deco press
ISSUE 8
NEW TYPE DESIGN
USD $45
A S Books
Information graphics
Bob Noorda Design
logo
7 GRIDS AMBROSE / HARRIS
WORLD OF logotypes
World of Logotypes
designing
Otl Aicher
Frank Stella A Retrospective
logolounge
logo
logolounge 2
TM
The Untold Stories Behind 29 Classic Logos
Mark Sinclair
Corporate Identity Manual
David E. Carter
murakami ego
MODERN MONOGRAMS
THINGS I HAVE LEARNED
STEFAN SAGMEISTER
LOGOTYPES OF THE WORLD
VITAMIN P 2
NEW PERSPECTIVES IN PAINTING
Designed in the USSR 1950 – 1989
logotype
LOGO DESIGN
TASCHEN
MARKS AND MONOGRAMS OF THE MODERN MOVEMENT 1875–1930
LANCE WYMAN: THE VISUAL DIARIES 1973–1982
DESIGNING DESIGN
KENYA HARA
TRADE MARKS & SYMBOLS
ANDO
TASCHEN
TRADEMARKS AND SYMBOLS OF THE WORLD
CCCP
COSMIC COMMUNIST CONSTRUCTIONS PHOTOGRAPHED
WORLD TRADEMARKS
LOGO MODERNISM
TASCHEN
Anton Stankowski 1925–1995
Ernst & Sohn

AMSTERDAM
ARTEZA
GAFFER POWER
DUCK TAPE
CARTWRIGHT & BUTLER
PRO
RICO DESIGN

And if you are to be creative in this space it is important you have your favorite tools. This means a healthy supply of your favorite pencils, your favorite pencil sharpener, sketchbooks, and tracing paper. As a logo designer, those are four items that you need to have all the time. It will take time to discover your favorites, but once you do keep them close by.

Generally speaking, I recommend the following:

Find pencils that are made by a reliable company. They shouldn't pull from the paper when you use them, and they should smell good. Make sure they are made of a good wood so that when you sharpen them you're left with a high-quality graphite.

Make sure your sketchbooks are light enough for transport, or purchase a couple different sketchbooks—a pocket-sized one for carrying around and a larger one for sketching in your studio.

Use a heavier stock tracing paper, perhaps 100 grams. I have learned that these result in a much cleaner look, photograph well, and are easier to move around without worrying about creasing or crumpling.

Besides your meaningful objects and your favorite tools, just make sure you are surrounded by elements that inspire you, including the music and art you love. All of this ensures your design studio is your creativity home.

A painting room; Studio George Bokhua

About the Author

Logo designer George Bokhua has more than fifteen years of experience in identity design and development. He has worked with a variety of clients all over the world, from small start-ups to established brands such as Disney, New Balance, NFL, Sonic, and *Wired* magazine.

Bokhua, who is well known for his simple, clean, sophisticated style and the use of grid systems and geometric shapes in his process, teaches three popular classes on Skillshare that serve as an introduction to his approach. To see more of his work, visit his Instagram account @george_bokhua. He lives in Tbilisi, Georgia.

Photo by Holger Mentzel

Acknowledgments

The book is dedicated to my daughter Ana and to my parents Manana Vekua and Merab Bokhua, whose support of my talents in childhood and through my adult years have driven me to get to where I am now.

Thanks to Maria Akritidou for assisting me with layouts and to Gika Mikabadze for providing articles for Chapter 2 “Are Logos Just Logos,” “1.618033,” “Rule or No Rule?” and “Less Is More?” Also special thanks to Natia Lursmanashvili for supporting me in this endeavor.

Index

Page numbers in *italic* indicate illustrations